Child of God

Child of God

by Kim Fraser

Illustrations by Sava Pinney

Child of God
Copyright © Kim Fraser 2006, 2007
First published in 2006 by Higher Guidance Pty Ltd, Australia
This edition published in 2007 by Findhorn Press

ISBN 978-1-84409-118-8

Nothing in this book should be construed as therapy or medical treatment. The ideas and suggestions in this book are meant to be used in
conjunction with regular medical treatment. When used properly, you
can ignite your spirit and find within the keys to personal fulfilment
and good health.

Cover design by Damian Keenan and Thierry Bogliolo
Illustrations by Sava Pinney (except for images and artwork on the following pages: 60, 62, 96, 102, 103, 118, 146)

A CIP catalogue record for this title is available from the British Library.

1 2 3 4 5 6 7 8 9 10 11 12 13 14 13 12 11 10 09 08 07

Published by
Findhorn Press
305a The Park, Findhorn
Forres IV36 3TE
Scotland, UK
Tel +44(0)1309-690582
Fax +44(0)1309-690036
eMail info@findhornpress.com
www.findhornpress.com

Contents

CHAPTER 6

**PART 5 Healing the Astral Body
using the Antakarana and Violet Flame** 141

CHAPTER 14

CHAPTER 15

CHAPTER 16

CHAPTER 17

Acknowledgements

To the plan of love and light, and those who guide us to achieve our highest destiny. For the wisdom flowing from my living teachers, I am truly grateful. Thank you to Raym and Master Choa Kok Sui for teaching me about the amazing world of energy and prana. Many blessings to Qala for her friendship, love and inspired teaching. To three great gurus, Sai Baba, Sri Jaya Nara and Sri Jaya Shakti, thank you for waking me up and guiding my soul.

To Barbara and Terry Tebo, thank you for starting me on the journey into awakening, and for teaching me about personal responsibility . Your wisdom is the foundation upon which I find emotional harmony if ever I am careless enough to lose it.

My partner, Hugh Keller, is a pillar of support, wisdom and encouragement. His spirituality and faith are inspirational, and his mental and emotional refinement give me something to emulate. He somehow manages to be distinguished, accomplished, playful and amusing all at the same time. Child of God and wise counsel, you are a gift indeed.

My children continue to blossom and unveil their pure and loving hearts. They are captivating, fun, deeply spiritual, honest and aware, and are greatly loved by the many people who comprise our extended families.

Many blessings to Sava for her inspired artwork, wit, drawings and friendship. Thank you to Gina White and Sally Carney for their assistance with editing and reading the manuscript of this book. To my fellow Harmony Centre directors, Hugh Keller, David Cole, John Steggles and Antoinette Sampson, I deeply appreciate your big hearts, faith and energy.

To everyone at The Harmony Centre, thank you for co-creating something really special. Warm thanks go to Sioux, a great healer and clairvoyant; to Chef Robert who spoils us; to Diane and Karen for their warmth and creativity, and to Liz my assistant who is the world's best manifester. To Amalie, Belinda, Kelly, Ginny, Greg(s) Yvonne, Brendan and everyone who visits and supports this sanctuary of the spirit. You are amazing, thank you.

Special thanks to all of the great teachers whose work has influenced me, and whom I have not met, such as His Holiness the Dalai Lama, Ram Dass, Dr Caroline Myss, Louise L. Hay, Sanaya Roman, Neale Donald Walsch, Alice Bailey and others.

To the readers of this book, may you discover the Divine child you are, and may that discovery bring you the immense joy and peace it has brought me.

Namaste. (I honour your divinity.)

Introduction

WELCOME TO PLANET EARTH

When we come to Earth you would think that we would be issued with a clear and useful instruction book so that life would proceed with ease and grace. Instead we get parents and an existing culture, and we remember nothing of where we have come from or why we are here. If this feels inadequate it is no use blaming your parents or even society, because they didn't receive an instruction manual either.

Once here, much of our time is occupied by the day to day requirements of making a living, falling in love, getting married, having kids, getting divorced, getting old, getting fit, paying the mortgage, and acquiring more, newer and better things. As a result, we often don't get around to thinking about the bigger questions, like where we came from and why we are here.

Even after achieving much of what I thought I was here to achieve, I reached a point where I wondered... is this all there is? Surely there must be more to life than this? At the time I was living a luxurious life as a barrister, but I still felt a little depressed, as though I had missed something important and I couldn't remember what it was. Having a baby put pressure on a shaky marriage, and I ended up going through a messy divorce, with all of the associated mental, emotional, financial challenges. I had a very young child and a demanding career, and nothing I had learnt prepared me for all this. It was a stressful, confusing and difficult time, and it drove me to look for answers in places I hadn't considered before.

This was the beginning of many years of diligent searching, and the discovery of the incredible depth and beauty of a Divine relationship. My consciousness expanded and I came to understand and experience concepts that I once would have scoffed at. For instance, who would have thought this formerly sceptical and analytical barrister would become clairvoyant? The more searching I did, the richer my life became. I found the most convincing and wonderful evidence of just how much more there is, and the meaning of my own life has become clearer. I am now calmer, more relaxed and more empowered. I feel happier and my life is better than it ever was. The material riches of my former life pale into insignificance next to the riches that I have found within.

WORLDS

What I have discovered is that I, like everyone else, am a multi-dimensional child of God. I have discovered whole worlds which exist beyond the physical one. My experiences of other dimensions have more or less matched teachings from mystics, gurus, and various sacred scriptures. These other worlds or dimensions offer rich gifts of understanding, and provide answers to why things happen in our physical world. This knowledge helps me to live a happy, balanced life.

I have sought in this book to simplify something that is often presented in either a very haphazard or very complex fashion. This book is a conversational user's guide to different parts of the self that will help you to achieve greater understanding, depth, peace, prosperity and a real and meaningful relationship with your Divine parents (God/Goddess). The final section of the book offers practical tools to help you free yourself from seen and unseen limitations in your consciousness, and will help you to discover your full potential.

MULTI-DIMENSIONAL EARTH

Undoubtedly there is more to life than what we can see, feel, touch, taste and smell using ordinary human physical senses. There are many important things that we cannot even classify as physical, like feelings, premonitions, friendships, love, attractions to some people and aversions to others.

Even within the physical dimension, humans can only see a limited colour spectrum, and can only hear a certain sound range frequency. We cannot see infra red light for instance, but we know it exists. There are certain dog whistles that humans cannot hear, while dogs can. There is so much of which we are unaware.

Just because most people are not conscious of the five dimensions that you are about to be lead through, does not mean that they do not exist. Many levels of consciousness exist, but the human consciousness apparatus, our brain, is normally incapable of perceiving them. There are so many helpful resources available to us beyond the physical dimension, and beyond our ordinary every day consciousness. There are conscious energy beings, angels for instance, that can help us solve problems, lead us to happiness, overcome our disappointments, create wonderful opportunities and heal conflicts.

The development of multi-dimensional consciousness will increase the range of things that you can know, understand, and make use of in your life. The bigger your awareness becomes, the more tools you will have at your disposal so that you can lead a life more filled with ease and grace.

If we look only at the physical world, only part of life can make sense. By seeing beyond the world of form and into the worlds of energy, we can recognize great patterns and states of being that make clear what spiritual teachers of all traditions have been telling people for eons. There really is a

God who loves us. We are Divine beings with immortal souls. Doing good things and forgiving others is actually good for you, and soon you will find out why. There is human law which, even to a lawyer, does not always make sense. There is also God's law, which is completely fair and embracing, loving and enabling.

I hope that this book will help you to see yourself in a whole new light, and awaken your spirit to the great adventure within, where you will find more than you ever thought possible. What you will find, if you take the time to look, is God[1].

---

[1]God has no gender and is beyond religion, so terms like God, Divine Energy, Cosmic Consciousness, Goddess, Divine Mother, Shiva and Allah are used interchangeably.

PART I
Multi-dimensional Me

Chapter 1

Huge support system

The physical world of people, places, things, events and time, take place at what could be described as the pointy end of a great unseen supporting structure. This structure includes many levels, and exists through different dimensions.

Many old spiritual books talk about the outer world of form (the physical dimension) and the inner world of the spirit. However, the inner world is not just a big space with stuff floating around in it. It is separated into different dimensions, and each dimension has different fundamental functions and structures.

There are five dimensions that humanity, at this point in our evolution, is heavily engaged with[2]. What is more, we each have five bodies corresponding to the five dimensions. These dimensions (and bodies) are:

1. **The Physical dimension**

2. **The Etheric dimension**

3. **The Astral dimension**

4. **The Soul dimension**

5. **The Divine dimension**

Each dimension operates differently and has a different set of rules. These are hidden, natural laws. You cannot hammer a nail into an (astral) idea, nor think your way through a (physical) solid wall. In the physical world we have the law of gravity and the concept of time. Neither of these things exists in any other dimension. In the astral world there is the law of polarity, which means that there is an opposite potential for all things. Instead of 'happy' we can have 'sad'. Instead of 'inspired' we can have 'dejected', and so on. Polarity also exists in the physical dimension where we can have 'overweight' and 'thin', 'up' and 'down'. Polarity is not present in the etheric, soul and Divine dimensions.

The laws above affect us here below in the physical dimension so we might as well learn how to work with them. By recognizing and using the different

---

[2] It is a mistake to believe that things beyond the physical realm are finite. There are endless dimensions, but they are so far removed from our everyday life that there is little point in talking about them. To say there are 5 dimensions is to provide a simplification of something vastly complex, so that it is understandable at this stage.

dimensional realities, we gain some insight into how we can shape our lives. It then becomes easier to achieve what we want to achieve, to have a more conscious connection with our creator, and thus a much better life.

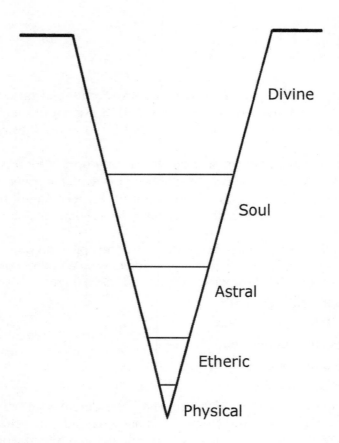

As you can see, the physical part might be the pointy end, but it is actually the smallest part of who we are. The physical dimension is the densest body that we have, and it includes our physical body and physical things in our universe.

The etheric body is very close to it, less dense but still able to be felt with the hands if you know how. It includes our aura, our chakras and the meridians that join everything together. This subject is covered in detail in my book, *Ignite Your Spirit*[3].

The astral dimension is less dense again, and is the dimension in which all of our thoughts, beliefs, memories, dreams and emotions occur. As a human

[3] Ignite Your Spirit by Kim Fraser, Higher Guidance Pty Ltd, Australia 2004, Brumby Books or through our website, www.kimfraser.com, Findhorn Press forthcoming.

your consciousness is engaged in this dimension most of the time. It contains the familiar stuff (for better or worse) that fills your mind.

The mind power movement of the last 50 years has contributed greatly to our consciousness of positive thinking and our ability to remove negative, fear-based beliefs. This shift in the astral dimension has brought positive changes and empowerment to many people. There is still a long way to go, and one of the great limitations is that it is still focuses on the mind, and how to use and control it. Making changes in our lives is more effective if we work in the soul and etheric dimensions, as well as the important astral dimension.

The astral dimension has no light source of its own, and relies on us to bring that light in from the soul and Divine dimensions. It can be a very confusing zone, where things are not always as they seem. The astral dimension is the biggest stumbling block to clarity and Divine oneness, so we will be spending quite a bit of time looking at how it works and how to master it.

The soul dimension is home, where we live when we are not physically and astrally embodied. It is eternal and huge, and is far less dense than the astral, etheric or physical parts of us.

Each person has a soul which never dies. Each soul is in the process of evolution, gaining wisdom and experience, different kinds of skills, and ever expanding consciousness. The journey of the soul is to become a perfected being of love, light, power and wisdom. The physical thing we think of as 'me' is just a part of the soul, in the same way that our finger is part of our hand.

Soul consciousness is very expansive compared to our usual mind consciousness. Through contact with our soul, it is possible to know things we have not actually learned before. Soul consciousness does not come through mind training, goal setting and logic, but through our intuition. Developing your intuition is therefore quite important. In addition to the methods we mentioned earlier, the fastest way to activate your intuition and gain Divine awareness is through development of your etheric body, particularly the heart chakra. We will look at this in some detail later in Chapter 9.

The Divine dimension is the ultimate everything. It is the Heart and Mind of God through which all things originate. It is like a void because it contains absolutely no matter. It is pure consciousness, the lightest and finest of the dimensions. It is from here that God gave birth to our souls.

We have a Divine spark within us called our monad. Monadic consciousness is really rare on Earth, however people like Jesus, Krishna, Mohammed, Sai Baba, Ammachi, and others, have developed themselves to such a degree that they can merge with God and survive. Not only can they hold this universal Christed energy, but they can assist others to do so through an energy transferral process which comes with vast spiritual development. Eventually every one of us will reach the level of development of these Great Souls in this life or another. The Divine plan says so.

Chapter 2

Seeing depends on where you are looking from

Imagine that you are in the physical tip of the V diagram. If you tried to look up and see the other dimensions from the physical world with your physical senses, then the etheric, astral and soul dimensions are invisible and empty. There is nothing there. People might even believe that they don't exist.

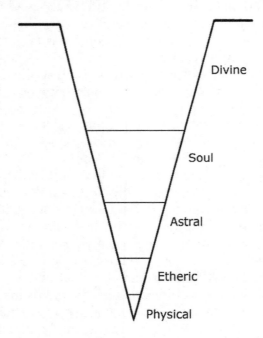

Looking down through the V diagram from the perspective of the Divine dimension, the other dimensions are teaming with life. Souls are clearly visible, brightly coloured lights which have their own sound and geometry. Angelic and Master beings of great love and wisdom who do not presently have physical, astral and etheric bodies, exist in this dimension. Through connecting with our own soul, we can communicate with them.

From the Divine and Soul perspectives, the astral dimension and the etheric dimension contain matter in a similar (but less dense) way to which the physical world does. In the astral dimension there are thoughts, emotions and various kinds of life that cluster around and inside any given physical person. With enhanced soul and Divine consciousness, beliefs, fears and thoughts are clairvoyantly and clairaudiently able to be seen and heard.

In the etheric world there are energy fields, chakras, meridians and various elemental beings including fire salamanders, water undines, air nymphs (also called fairies) and earth elementals. These beings tend the physical world and are prolific in areas of clean and un-spoilt earth. Humans generally feel good when they visit pristine natural places because the energy is so rich. Elemental beings of nature are less numerous in areas built up by humans, such as in cities.

The idea of unseen universes may seem ridiculous to those whose consciousness is limited to the physical world. As we start to develop our consciousness beyond the boundary of the purely physical senses, the idea that there is 'nothing else' is just as ridiculous. When you achieve a degree of conscious soul connection, you can see into the other dimensions for yourself.

Chapter 3

Carrot and Stick Motivation

The pull towards Divine oneness is strong and inescapable. The joy of Divine connection can be sufficient incentive of itself to motivate you to keep going. It is like a carrot dangled before us encouraging us to move forward. However, when we either deliberately or through inadvertence turn away from the Goddess, less Divine energy can permeate our life and things can start to go wrong. This has nothing to do with punishment.

What we focus on grows. If we focus on Divine things and cultivate love, joyfulness, happiness and peace, we pull ourselves towards God even if we don't believe in him. If we focus on stress, anxiety, problems, imperfections and what others are doing wrong, we create more of these experiences, and bring less love, joy, happiness and peace into our lives. Consequently we move away from wholesome awareness and forget that we really are Divine children of God.

Everything in our life is there to help us realize that our ultimate reality is Divine oneness. When we experience flow, coincidences, happiness and synchronicity, we are on track with conscious soul union and our progress can be easy and graceful. When we experience hardship, conflict, pain and various types of suffering or deprivation, we are not actually on the path of ease and grace, but on some other path to Divine oneness. This is when the universal stick comes out to prod us forward. It didn't have to be this way, it was our choice.

The loving forces of creation allow us freedom of direction, and choice of path. We are offered easy ways forward and hard ways forward. Many of us choose really hard paths, which bring us to a place where we have to surrender what we thought our life was about, so as to pay attention to what the unseen part is up to. Illness, accident, divorce, failure and unpleasant karma of various kinds, are all balancing factors which will, one way or another, ensure that we return into the majesty of Divine oneness, whichever way we choose.

ALMA

Alma was an older woman who came to me very ill with pancreatic cancer. She had been on chemotherapy which did not destroy her large tumour. During the healing, I asked her what she thought she had learned from her cancer. She looked at me as though I was mad. Then she started to cry, and spoke about how her life had completely changed because of her condition.

Alma had been a really angry woman. As a child she had been a war refugee, having left Poland with her family. Her relationship with her husband was stormy because Alma could not contain her anger. Prior to her cancer, she had been a worrier and very concerned about money. She had been critical of her adult children and there were rifts between various family members. She was not a particularly spiritual person.

Because of her illness, Alma had softened and changed. She had become very close to her daughters, and their hearts had opened fully to each other. She was not concerned about anything other than her own health, and the wellbeing of the people she loved. She had learned the importance of love, and of appreciating every day. Through healings with various people she had released a lot of stored anger, and was learning how to deal differently now with her emotions.

Alma's gratitude for all of the things she had in her life was immense. She no longer ruminated about what she did not have, but gave thanks for what she did have. The healings she experienced opened her to the feeling of Divine energy, and she had become very devotional, believing deeply in Jesus and Mother Mary. In short, she was completely transformed by the experience.

The cancer energy had felt to me like an unpleasant electrical current running through her aura and navel chakra. Alma was able to thank the spirit of the cancer for being with her and helping her grow. It completely lifted out of her body. She felt intense tingling at the site of the tumour, and we both knew she was going to be fine. The cancer had done its job, and Alma understood. She had turned her whole life towards deep respect, love and gratitude, all of which are soul characteristics. She was on her way to conscious Divine union, and her health could now improve.

No random events

Not every cancer is a result of suppressed emotions. Serious illness usually has a karmic element to it, as we shall see later. The seed of a condition such as cancer may have been planted in a former incarnation. There is no blame attached or intended in this analysis, only a means of empowerment. When we can accept that events are not random but are created by our choices and our past history, we can isolate the cause of the problem. Sometimes that problem is to do with our physical behaviour, but often it is beyond that. Through increasing our understanding of other dimensions of reality, we have more places to look for solutions.

Provided we have sufficient reservoirs of Divine grace, events can be altered for the better through Divine connection.

Nothing up my sleeve...

From a Buddhist perspective, all of physical reality is a big illusion called Maya, conjured up by the thoughts, beliefs and karma of humans[4]. Our dense physical reality is only as 'real' as we believe it to be. When you start to work with your astral body, you will see for yourself that our experience of life on

---

[4] There are many books written on the mind power theme, showing us how, if we change our thinking our whole world changes. One of the best of these books is by Florence Scovel Shinn, written in 1925. It is called *The Game of Life and How to Play it*. This little book is a rare gem simply written and clearly expressed. If you are not yet familiar with the concept that we create our own physical reality through our thoughts and beliefs, this is the book for you.

Earth is just a reflection of our beliefs, individually and collectively. It can all be changed as we choose different beliefs and behaviour.

There is a wonderful film called *"What the Bleep do we Know"*, in which a group of scientists and quantum physicists explain and graphically illustrate the scientific basis for this proposition, which is based in quantum mechanics. They say that there is endless energy and potential that is not manifest. This energy will warp and bend in accordance with our beliefs, and become reality. This is the same as saying that pure energy (the Divine dimension) registers our thoughts (astral dimension) and causes them to come into creation (physical dimension). The conduit pipe through which this happens is our etheric body.

It is very hard for humans to accept the reality that everything around us is just energy that is either static, or in motion. The chair you sit on is only a chair in the physical dimension, and only for a period of time. It didn't exist before, and it won't exist in a thousand years. The energy that comprised it will. The chair is just part of 'Maya' or the 'illusion of reality'.

Maya is seductively ensnaring, and the fact that physical reality resulting from Maya is so solid that you can kick it, does not change the fact that things are the way they are in our life because we (and Society, our tribe) believe they will be.

Trying out the theory of maya
against a brick wall..

Even when we understand the concept of Maya, and actually understand that not much is real except that you believe it, it is still hard not to be drawn into the illusion. As soon as we change our core beliefs, startling changes in the world around us can occur, as happened with Selena.

SELENA

Selena was an aspiring actress who was about to star in a local amateur the-atrical production. In a bid to progress her career, she called up many agents to see whether they would come and watch the show, to see her perform with a view to representing her in the future. After many said 'no', one said 'yes' and came to a rehearsal evening. The agent however, only had eyes for the young male lead, and all of her conversation was directed toward him. All she said to Selena about her performance was, "Have you been professionally trained?" As Selena had spent 4 years getting a degree in acting and had, prior to the birth of her child, done quite a bit of work in the field, she was devastated. She thought she should just give up and not embarrass herself further.

When Selena came to see me she was depressed and on the verge of ending her career. When I looked clairvoyantly at Selena's beliefs, the primary one was, "I am not good enough". It was huge and looming over her. Given that our thoughts create our reality, Selena was busy creating failure as an actress as part of hers.

I cleaned up Selena's aura and chakras[5], and then helped her dissolve the belief using energy healing techniques from chapter 16 in this book. We then replaced the thought with:

"I Selena am a fantastic actress, well loved and respected by myself and others".

What happened afterwards was truly amazing. She had no sooner left the healing room than her phone rang, and it was the agent asking her to come in for an interview. She told Selena that she thought that her role was not allowing her to display her true potential, but that she definitely had talent and that there would be scope for many other roles.

By changing the basic thought she was holding, Selena changed her entire physical reality. She scored herself an agent, and within days was offered roles in forthcoming plays.

---

[5] Using a form of healing called Ignite Your Spirit, explained in detail in my first book *Ignite Your Spirit*. Parts of this technique are also explained later in this book. The aura and chakras form part of the etheric body, an important part of who we are in terms of soul connection.

Miracles

How did this happen? Selena stopped using logic, which says that most actresses are out of work and struggling. Instead she started to use her creative potential, accessed through her intuition combined with a clean energy (etheric) body. Her Soul (Higher Self) was instantly able to change her reality because she had removed her former blocking belief. She could then enjoy a better life experience.

As you open to your soul and Divine self, you raise your consciousness. By raising our consciousness, we open to new ways of looking at old problems. Albert Einstein said,

"We cannot solve our problems with the same thinking we used when we created them."

By deliberately expanding our awareness, we can achieve a better world for ourselves and others, and move further into the understanding of our rich Divine heritage.

Chapter 4

Human Consciousness

"As soon as you lift up your consciousness to the state of Divine Awareness, you see the oceanic current of God's light flowing Behind all matter. You see everything in terms of spirit."

Paramahansa Yogananda

A lot of our education and focus, in terms of developing the mind, has to do with developing our ability to think logically and rationally. Rational thinking is very important and fundamental to dealing with physical events and choices. However, contrary to what some might think, rational thinking is not the peak experience in consciousness even though it is wonderful and useful. It is not possible to experience Divine consciousness through use of the rational mind and through rational analysis. All rationality can do is develop theories of what God or unseen universes might be like.

To really know what is going on, we need to develop other parts of our thinking ability. First, we need to develop the ability to be intuitive. Then we go beyond the mind altogether, and open into the boundless light of love wisdom that exists beyond all form.

A nice girl like me

By virtue of having a good education, including degrees in economics and law and 16 years practice as a barrister, I was fortunate enough to develop a certain degree of rational thinking. When I began my spiritual training, there was a point where I had to admit that my strong logical mind could not provide me with answers to some pretty important questions. For instance, it could not help me understand how to be happy, and was seemingly of little use in having a close and loving intimate relationship. It could not see any rational argument for the existence of angels, souls, Divine beings, nor could it answer the big question as to whether or not there was a God. Given what I knew at the time, there seemed to be logical arguments for and against such a big proposition.

Rational thinking relies upon there being a stable paradigm or set of parameters in which it can operate. Within those parameters, rational thinking serves us well. When things change, when events happen that are not programmed into the paradigm or when emotional responses occur, rational thinking alone might not be able to provide us with answers as to how to move forward.

The human design is that intuitive consciousness gives us access to the big picture of what is going on in our lives. Rational consciousness shows us how to formulate and implement plans to achieve what the intuitive part wants, and to correlate our awareness with living on earth.

Rational and intuitive thought are carried out, roughly speaking, in two different sides of the brain. Split brain experiments conducted on epileptics in the 1950s showed that the two sides of the brain operate somewhat differently and independently of each other.

Left brain

The left side of the brain is rational and linear. It likes things to happen in an orderly sequence. The left side of our brain can understand time, which is a function of the physical world. It is also logical, and can do math, solve equations and deduce 'If this, then that', in the way that a binary computer does. It is ordered and analytical, and thinks in words because it is language oriented.

Isaac Newton's view of the world, which is the cornerstone of scientific thought, is heavily rational and relies on a mechanistic world view in which things can be dissected and understood.

The left brain is very yang (male). This means that it is active and projects itself in a 'doing' way. If you think of the archetypal married couple of old, the man goes off to work to do business while the woman stays home and does the nurturing, child raising and feels her emotions. The man is trained to have a stiff upper lip and to suppress emotions (which are intuitive or right brain).

The rational left brain wants to approach the world in a way that has things in nice, neat, understandable boxes. It loves ordered sequences, and tends to break everything down into parts in order to understand it.

This approach is good for getting things done, however it leaves many important questions unanswered. When it dominates the right brain, it can lead to a quality of life in which certain key elements such as good health, warm, intimate relationships, happiness, love and Divine experiences are conspicuously absent.

In our culture both men and woman have become very left brain oriented. In the East there is a much stronger right brain understanding of life. This is reasonably frustrating to the rational perspective, but perfect for the circumstances. I am convinced that driving a car on roads in India is only possible if one suspends logic and enters into unity consciousness with all the other drivers on the road. There seem to be no parameters, the only rule there is: there are no rules!

The problem with rational thinking is that it relies on parameters which may or may not be accurate for its validity. Logical rational thinking is a great servant, but it can be addictive, and prevent one from exploring outside of the boundaries inherent in the paradigm of life from which it flows. The current obsession with rational thinking prevents awareness of the rich and extended array of consciousness that is possible.

Right brain

The right side of the brain is far more able to grasp soul connection and the whole idea of multi-dimensionality. It is artistic, musical, intuitive, creative and feeling oriented. The right brain is able to tune into spiritual experiences and into our physical body. It wants us to have fun.

The right brain is very receptive and instead of moving in a linear way, it moves in a 'whole picture' way. Everything affects everything else and makes the 'whole' different. The right brain has gestalt intelligence, which means it sees the big picture, and therefore has no need to break something up to understand it. It is actually faster getting to a result than the left brain, which has to process a number of steps to establish an outcome. The left brain is results oriented while the right brain is interested in the journey. How we do it is more important to the right brain than what we do or where we go with it.

The right brain thinks in pictures, symbols and sensations. The unseen, artistic, musical, spiritual and mystical parts of life are very real to those with right brain development.

Each side of the brain has a different agenda, and in most people one side is dominant over the other.

Most well educated westerners are strongly left brain dominant. For these people the intuitive, multi-dimensional world is a bit of a mystery which seems too illogical to even seriously contemplate. This is a problem for the unbalanced left brain dominant person, and for all of society because it stops us from expanding into our full potential, individually and collectively.

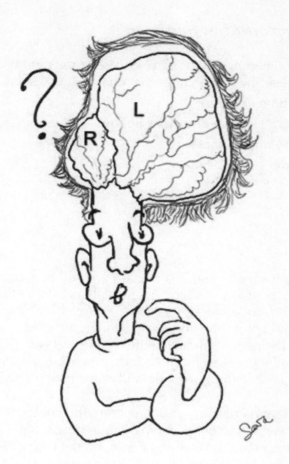

Achieving conscious Divine connection

Achieving soul connection and the realization of your own divinity is not possible through the logical left brain. The right brain gives us the intuitive pathways for soul connection, but eventually we go beyond the mind altogether and achieve true higher consciousness. To start with, we need to develop our intuitive faculty and our ability to use the right brain.

When I started my spiritual journey, my left brain was huge and my right brain was about the size of a pea in terms of its usefulness. I cannot paint or draw to save myself. I dropped out of piano lessons when I was 8 years old and never thought of myself as someone who was in the least bit intuitive. Over time and through deliberate development of my intuition, many things have changed. I have worked at developing intuition. I still cannot draw, but I have learnt how to be clairvoyant, clairsentient, musical, telepathic and aware of Higher Guidance. It took time and work to make these changes, but if I can do it, with a bit of application, so can you.

How to develop intuitive thinking

There are many different ways to develop use of the right brain and intuitive thinking processes. The 5 main ones that I have found useful are:

1. **Spend time in nature**
2. **Take up a creative or artistic hobby**
3. **Listen to or play music**
4. **Meditate**
5. **Relax**

Nature

Energy in a city is usually fairly haphazard and full of activity. Thousands or even millions of people thinking thoughts, talking, doing things, along with traffic, noise, and pollution etc combine to create a thick soup of energy. When we go into nature the energy is different. In a forest for instance, the energy is more harmonious. Imagine the feeling you get when you walk into an old forest that has existed for thousands of years. It is tranquil, serene and timeless. There is something relaxing and rejuvenating about these types of places.

Mountains have particularly strong energy. The energy is lighter, as is the air itself. The ocean is another place that brings peace to people and changes their energy. Remember the feeling of being at the beach? It is relaxing and calming. The more you connect to nature the more your intuitive mind gets stimulated.

Hobby and creativity

Any kind of creative hobby will assist you to access and develop your right brain, so long as you enjoy it. It helps if you do not have to do it for a linear purpose, like making money, and if it doesn't have to be done under strict time limitations. Building model train sets, knitting, painting, pottery, sport and many other things can help us relax and activate our creative and intuitive juices.

Music and sound

Music is very good for activating creativity, Divine connection and the right brain. When you are choosing what music to listen to, be aware of the overall vibration of the music. Is it wholesome and uplifting, or is it full of head banging, smashing noises and negative sentiments? It has been proven by a Japanese scientist that different types of music affect the integrity of water, causing it to form different types and shapes of water crystals when it is frozen and examined under a microscope. Heavy metal music causes the crystals to shatter and explode outwards. Chanting and classical music such as Mozart, causes beautiful crystals to form, even in horrible, polluted water that usually has poor crystal formation. Why is this relevant to you? Because your body is comprised of over 70% water.

Think what you are doing to yourself with the music you listen to. Are you ripping your water molecules apart, or creating harmony and serenity internally? A picture is worth a thousand words. To really see what I mean, go to the website of www.hado.com where various copyrighted photographs are displayed.

Meditation

Meditation is somewhat more complex than the other three methods of right brain activation. Because of the general lack of understanding of what it means to meditate, I have written a separate book about how to do it. In our workshops we show people how it is done, and it brings huge changes to the lives of those who practise. Regular meditation is jam packed with advantages including stress management, better health, more energy and vitality and inner peace. Over time, it brings with it soul consciousness and a better developed intuition. It is one of the most amazing ways to bring lasting change to your life, so why not give it a go?

To be shaken out of the ruts of ordinary perception, to be shown for a few timeless hours the outer and inner world, not as they appear to an animal obsessed with survival or to a human being obsessed with words and notions, but as they are apprehended, directly and unconditionally, by Mind at Large - this is an experience of inestimable value to everyone...

Aldous Huxley, The Doors of Perception, 1954

Relax

Do you spend much time just doing nothing in particular? Most of us don't. We race around trying to fit more activity into seemingly shorter spaces of time. This is not conducive to intuitive awareness.

Find some time each day, even if only for a few minutes, to just relax. Don't read, don't plan, don't do anything. Just breathe and let your thoughts flow through. Just be. This is the difference between being a 'human being' as opposed to a 'human doing'.

PART 2
The Divine and Soul Dimensions

Chapter 5

The Divine Dimension

"The ultimate proof of God's existence will come
through your own experience in meditation.
Once you have found Him
In the cathedral of silent meditation
In the depths of your soul,
you will find Him everywhere".

Paramahansa Yogananda

God: Who?

The biggest part of our support system on Earth is the Divine dimension, the level of the unifying and transcendent spirit. The Holy Ghost, God the Father, the Creative Force, Nirvana, Shiva, Allah, Universal Intelligence, Holy Spirit, God the Mother, Goddess, YHWH… these and other words are used by Humanity to describe the essence of this level. It is the Alpha and the Omega, the beginning and the end, and everything exists within it.

God/Goddess is everywhere all of the time (omnipresent) and of course is capable of anything, literally omnipotent. No problem is too big or small for God. God doesn't have problems, just answers to ours.

What does God look like?

When I was a child I had the impression, which flowed from the teachings of the Catholic priests and nuns at school, that God was an old and stern man who lived in the clouds. He watched everything I did, so I had better be good!

God doesn't look like anything. Divine just is, like a huge invisible force field of energy, love and absolute intelligence. God has no form until God decides to make and take form. At that stage, other dimensions come into being through which sound, light and sacred geometry combine with varying degrees of consciousness, to form whatever is in the mind of God. God unfolds itself through all dimensions and all universes, and is inherent in all things within them.

Anything with a form is not part of this dimension, which is more like a sacred, nurturing, enfolding void. It is hard for humans, whose consciousness is intimately bound up in the senses, to conceive of Holy nothing. Divine forms (usually with personalities) such as Zeus, Ganesh, Athena and many others, have been ascribed to God/Goddess to give people something visible to worship in many spiritual traditions and cultures.

Yin and Yang

God has no gender and includes both polarities in unified form. The balance of yin and yang is able to be seen in the Hindu tradition, where the forces of Shakti and Shiva are said to comprise the whole of the Universe. Shiva, or God in unmanifest form, is seen as male (yang) or the active Divine principle. Shakti is God in manifest form. This is seen as female, or the receptive (yin) Divine principle. Shiva pours life (Divine energy) into Shakti, who receives it, giving birth to life and form in the physical world. Shiva could not do that without Shakti, the Goddess, who receives that energy and makes everything happen. She births everything, and nurtures and provides for it. At the essential core of this understanding is the fact that they are actually one.

No Thing There

This dimension is Divine, unmanifest awareness. It is the invisible orchestrating principle that caused everything to come into creation. Here there is no thing, no actual matter. At this level everything is pure consciousness, existing in unity and balance. There is just love and creative potential.

Everything including galaxies, souls and the things in our life, sprang from here. It is the Divine unmanifest storehouse of everything. It is inside us. It is what we are made of. We are it. It just is, it never began, never stops, and there is no end to that which is potentially able to flow from here, because of the infinite nature of God.

Eve and the apple

When things and souls come into being they take on matter. They fall into different dimensions, where certain rules apply. Then there is a long road back into the purity and perfection of existence in the state of Divine oneness again. It is all part of the grand plan, and part of the way in which creation keeps evolving.

Earlier I referred to Shakti and Shiva, and how it is the feminine principle that embodies manifest form and causes things to come into being.

It is no accident that the biblical account has Eve (the feminine) and not Adam eating the fruit of the tree of knowledge. It is no accident that the fruit is an apple, not a mandarin or an orange. The apple is long associated with the Goddess, as is the pentangle, the number five and the transit of Venus through the heavens (the only feminine planet, the rest are male). That transit looked at from Earth, describes a pentacle as it passes back and forth around the earth.

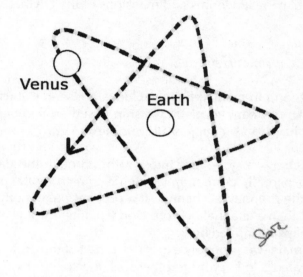

Cut an apple in half through the core horizontally, and you will see five segments. The early writers were veiling sacred knowledge in a myth. They were really talking about the feminine energy of Shakti, causing creation to come into being, not a woman causing the downfall of a man.

The tree of knowledge involves us in thinking. Thinking is an astral activity. By eating from the tree of knowledge, Eve fell from the dimension she and Adam were already in. They were already individuated and identifiable, so they had already come into the soul dimension, which could be called the Garden of Eden. They fell into the Astral and consequently, the physical dimension. The astral dimension exists in polarity (eg, good and bad, happy and sad) as does the physical dimension (up and down, rich and poor). Here in this dimension which mankind chose to enter, for the first time humanity discovered separateness to God, as well as pleasure and pain, success and failure, joy and suffering. Here is the greatest learning and fastest soul development of any place in the many kingdoms and mansions of the Divine.

Why God is seen as Male

In ancient times and in many religions, God is not seen exclusively as male. There is evidence of many forms of worship based on *feminine* concepts of deity. You only have to visit ancient historic sites in Europe and other places to see that.

Spiritual teachings may be cast into a form, through the distortion of the recipient that is partially correct, but which is tainted by the personal issues and beliefs of the prophet or channel. If a prophet believes that women are second to men, then a channeling from God will filter through the lens of that belief and perhaps be tainted by it.

That God is male was probably expected as part of the astral makeup of the men who 'revealed' God's word to other less developed people. Revelation of things from the Divine and Soul dimensions is always subject to the state of purity and stillness of the astral and etheric bodies of the person who taps into the higher consciousness. Cultural beliefs, which are astral phenomena, shape the revelation to the level of awareness and development of the people who are receiving Divine communication from God. The human prophet or emissary is not trying to mislead, they are simply incapable of conceiving of something that does not fit with their existing belief structures. Further, if they brought through a message that bore no relationship to the beliefs of those to whom they would be *revealing* God's words, they would not be able to communicate in a way that got the message out.

As the consciousness of humanity and our belief structures evolve, so too can our understanding of God. My own experience and that of the Gurus who have instructed me, is that God/Goddess is genderless, endless, vast, and personally loving, all at the same time.

Unconditional and Infinite

The very nature of God is unconditional love, deep peace, bliss, joyfulness and freedom. God is also infinite intelligence, which by definition is beyond our finite minds. Humans have, at various times in history, been recipients of Divine revelation. People have a tendency to think in *concrete* terms rather than in abstract and infinite ways. Thus, they assume that if they are right, then everyone else who disagrees with them is wrong. The word of God comes to them through this lens, and so they interpret it as if it says "and this is the right way and the only way that everyone should worship God".

The 'you have to do it this way' approach is unlikely to flow from pure Divine energy. "I will only love you if you do it my way" is a condition. If God loves us unconditionally, then God would not impose such a term. Conditionality is a negative gloss put on to information that is received. Even if the rest of a spiritual transmission or scripture is a true reflection, any part that does not resonate with unconditional love, kindness, tolerance and patience, is likely to be an example of astral interference.

Level of Interconnectedness

On our V diagram, the Divine dimension is not bounded at the top because it is infinitely huge and could never be fenced in. The Divine dimension is not bounded at all, and the whole V of you and me exists within it. The Divine dimension stretches from us, to everyone, through all time, through space and through all dimensions.

The horizontal lines at the top of the V are there to remind us that, at the level of the Divine dimension, we are all interconnected.

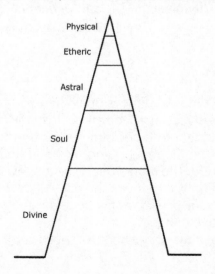

If we invert the V diagram, it could be seen as a wave poking up out of an ocean. Each person is like an individual wave on a giant ocean of consciousness, and eventually the wave merges back into the ocean again.

If everyone could be represented diagrammatically as a V, then through the unbounded Divine part we are all interconnected and one. Our unity is symbolized by the outreaching horizontal lines which are like hands stretching out to hold hands with the next person, totally interconnected. Each of us helps the other to manifest the life that we believe in, and have incarnated to experience. At this level, we truly are one.

You are perfect already

We are already divine by our very design, by our essence and our heritage. God truly is our mother and father, and so we are Divine children of God. The limitations on our consciousness prevent us from remembering this. Remembering our Divine history involves opening our consciousness more than before. Holy Saints and spiritual Masters know themselves to be Divine. Through their loving and personal relationship with the Divine, they are often capable of doing things that we would regard as miraculous. They are merely activating laws from other dimensions, and using them to achieve certain outcomes in the physical world.

There is a bit of this Divine energy in every molecule in the universe. This means that everyone and everything is a part of the continuous expression of the Divine dimension. Even though I am using a 5 dimensional system to explain multi-dimensionality, at the level of the Divine dimension, it is all one (in fact, this is the ultimate reality). It is all just conscious energy, and all of it, including you and me and all of the dimensions are a part of it. All of what we see as imperfect is actually meant to be, and perfect in itself.

Time

Time only exists in the physical dimension. When you try to solve problems through physical means, it can take a long time. In many circumstances, things can be 'sped up' by going into other dimensions and working on solutions there. Whatever occurs on the inner plane, will end up becoming visible (in time) in the physical world. The more your conscious awareness is attached to the physical dimension only, the slower the pace of development and change can be. The more that your conscious awareness expands, the more it seems that time is only a relative thing.

Einstein proved that time is relative to speed and distance. Have you noticed that when you are busy or having a good time, time goes quickly and when you are bored, time goes slowly? Our consciousness has an effect upon our experience of everything, including time.

I once narrowly avoided a very serious car accident. I was driving home from a very stimulating spiritual development seminar. I was thinking about the things we had been taught and my consciousness was more expanded than it had been previously.

There was light to moderate traffic and I was travelling 80 kilometres an hour on a busy 6 lane road in Sydney, when a sudden and awful accident two cars ahead of me occurred. The car in front of me crashed into the back of the first two cars and I really had nowhere to go and no physical means of avoiding the collision.

Then the strangest thing happened. It was as though time slowed down and I saw the pieces of steel and glass flying up into the air as though they were in slow motion. I had plenty of time to check behind me, and swerve through the flying debris and the spinning cars. Once I was through the situation and further down the road, time resumed its usual speed. Somehow time itself had come to my rescue, slowing down and giving me plenty of time to be safe and on my way.

When you make connections beyond the physical dimension, you put in place safety belts that can help you when you need it, providing you have sufficient karmic grace to activate them. Outside of the physical dimension, the only time there is, is now.

Does God really answer prayers?

God answers every single prayer, very efficiently. As soon as you pray for anything at all, the energy for it is sent to you. Universes spin around your prayer in an effort to answer it.

If you pray for peace and happiness, the energy of it has already been sent to you. If you pray for a solution to a problem you have, the solution is thereby brought into existence in the Divine dimension, straight away.

While it does not take God long to answer our prayers, it can take us a long time to be in an appropriate state, multi-dimensionally speaking, to receive God's blessings. This can result in a time lag between the formation of our prayer, and receipt of the physical result. We can actually be blocked from the ability to receive the blessing, even though we want it. This is not due to external factors as we might imagine, but because of blockages in our soul, etheric and astral bodies. These act as dams preventing the grace of God from pouring into the dimension where you want it, the physical one, where you are experiencing your life.

Understanding your multi-dimensionality will help you to break down the dam walls and allow Divine grace to flow to you. Through this you can create heaven on Earth. Special tools to help the process along are dealt with later in this book and in my book *Dimensions of Wealth*[6].

When we are energetically and astrally clear and ready, our life circumstances can change wondrously in the blink of an eye, such is the power and creativity of God.

What is God like?

To come into consciousness of the Divine is to enter into formlessness and unity consciousness. It is a blazingly blissful, alive, loving and accepting experience.

If you have some non-physical experience that you think is God, and there is any feeling of being judged, or there is fear or discomfort, it is not genuine. You are having a strong and unpleasant astral experience.

Experiences in the Divine realm are a mixture of unending ecstasy, combined with a sense of nothingness. Common to all truly Divine experiences is the feeling of there being only one; no subject being examined and no object doing the examining. Here there is a continuity of consciousness, awareness and love. It is indescribable. If you are looking at a tree, there is no tree and no sense of yourself as the 'you' doing the looking, there is just continual awareness. It is really difficult to describe exactly what it is like. It is bliss beyond words and form. You just have to experience it for yourself.

Earth: Why are we here?

Every religion has its own creation myths to explain why we came out of the oneness. Myths on the whole are started by incredibly wise spiritual teachers. They hide deep spiritual reality inside stories, so that those who are aware will find them, and those who are not aware will think they are just stories.

Creation myths are the attempts of incarnated humans (whose consciousness is, by design, limited) to understand how and why we are here.

In the ancient Greek and Roman traditions, a family of Gods caused things to occur. In the Shinto tradition there was a good female God with a nasty brother, and their relationship caused the events of the world. In the Christian tradition we have the story of Genesis. American Indians, Australian Aboriginals and the Celts all have their own ways of expressing how we came to be.

---

[5] Forthcoming title by the author. *Dimensions of Wealth* is also an experiential seminar which activates the participants and creates breakthroughs in energy and thought.

Science, which many people worship, has established that evolution has also caused part of the creative process. Recently discovered archaeological evidence, coupled with more precise methods of dating ancient relics, artefacts and human remains, have opened up speculation about accepted theories related to our origins.

Science is wonderful and has contributed amazing things to our enjoyment and quality of physical life. However science can be manifestly wrong as often as it is right. All you have to do is study scientific history to see this. If you are interested in anthropology and ancient history, have a look at Uriel's Machine by Christopher Knight and Robert Lomas.

These various mythological perspectives attempt to describe great cosmological events. It may be impossible to describe them through current human understanding. Some people mock others' theories, but if you look at the essence of the stories rather than the form, it is likely that there is some validity to most of them.

Blind man's elephant

Understanding the Divine mind from where we are here on earth, is even worse than the proverbial 10 blind men fighting over the proper description of an elephant. One man feels the trunk and says, "Elephants are curved, with a hole in the end. I know because I have felt it myself." Another says, "That is rubbish, elephants have hair on the end." (He felt the tail). One has felt the leg and says, "You are wrong, elephants are like palm trees." Another who felt the ears says, "You are all wrong. Elephants are flat and wave in the breeze." And so on.

Neale Donald Walsch[7] has a really appealing theory of how it all came about. He says that God might already be everything, but existing in an unmanifest state, God could not experience anything. Thus, God split into parts, through which creation occurred. Worlds and universes were created through the use of Divine energy.

Dimensions, an endless geometry of light and dark, and the relationship between the two, allows for an infinite variety of life and experience. As God/Goddess is inherent in all, she gets to experience herself. God invented the physical world of Earth, along with various life forms, including humans, to inhabit it. Walsh claims that God continues to become more aware, through the unfolding of creation, and through the countless experiences that billions of humans have during their unique lifetimes.

---

[7] Conversations with God, book one two and three, but especially book one.

I separated myself from Myself
So that I may love Myself
See in Me Yourself.
For I see myself in All of You
You are my life, my breath, my soul
You are all my forms.
When I love you I love Myself
When You love Yourself, You love Me

Sai Baba, speaking of the nature of the Divine, 1998.

Be open and discriminating

It is impossible to fit Divine anything into a human physical mindset. If you want to know more about God, what you need to develop is your awareness, not theories (that are astral). As your consciousness expands, you will, through direct experience, increase your spiritual awareness. At the same time, it is important to develop discrimination, or accuracy of perception. The astral world can warp our perceptions. If a supposedly Divine experience or communication is not filled with love, it is astral, not Divine, and you are best to disengage from it.

With a little insight, you will recognize that your own perception of matters to do with God might be quite different from the next person. That does not make either of you wrong. It simply attests to the magnificent variety of experiences that humans are capable of having. Everyone experiences the Divine in their own way, in accordance with their individual level of consciousness.

Spiritual IQ

Just as there is a bell curve describing IQ or intelligence, so there is a bell curve describing spiritual development and Divine awareness.

At one end, there are people who have absolutely no interest or engagement in any form of spirituality. In the middle are people who have some awareness and follow some kind of spiritual instruction or religion. For these people much remains unexplained and uncomprehended. At the other end, God/ Goddess takes form on Earth at various times, in answer to the prayers of people for help and guidance.

Divine/Man forms are called Avatars. They have physical, etheric and astral bodies, but their consciousness is not limited like other humans. They are one in consciousness with the Divine, and this is what makes them so special. Jesus, Krishna and Sai Baba are examples of Avatars. They are aware of their Divine consciousness since birth.

As well as Avatars, there are people who are super achievers, who are astounding in their understanding and connection with the Divine. They are not born enlightened but become so through diligent spiritual study, building on past life spiritual development and becoming self realized in this one. These enlightened, God realized beings, are able to assist others to achieve God realization. They are devoted to making the world a better place and are known as saints, Buddhas or Gurus.

A Guru means a teacher who brings light to the darkness. The reality of Guru has nothing to do with the actual physical form of the teacher. It has to do with the Divine consciousness that the teacher is one with. They are great mentors.

One Guru I know says "Divine I am, but no more Divine than you." The difference is, most people don't actually know this, while the Guru knows and lives it. A true Guru does not seek power over others. They are consciously connected to our omnipotent parents, so power is something they have plenty of already. Guru, a human embodiment of Divine consciousness, seeks to empower and educate the people around them, to liberate their own latent potential.

If you read the lives of Gurus, saints and Avatars, you will find amazing examples of how they have helped those around them.

Heavy ∂uty energy

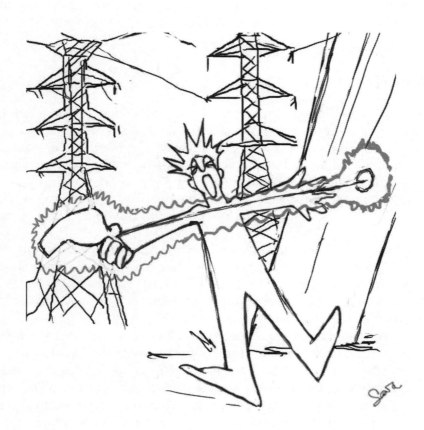

Divine consciousness is pure and loving, wise and blissful. It is very powerful and so is quite hard (even uncomfortable) for someone to grasp who has never tried. It can be tricky because it is of a very high 'voltage'.

Imagine that a human is equivalent to a household appliance, in terms of their ability to handle and make use of energy. 240 volts is just right. Imagine that the astral dimension runs at anywhere between 1 and 500 volts, the soul dimension runs at about 11,000 volts and God is at 33,000 volts and more. If we plug straight into our Divine self without prior preparation and without gearing up to do so, it can be too much energy and can overwhelm us.

We have a set of transformers that step energy down from the Divine dimension through the soul, then through the Earth itself, and finally into an energy stream that our etheric and physical bodies can safely handle. These are our chakras. Normally we only speak of 7 major chakras, but many more exist above our heads and below our feet, joining us into universal awareness. The chakras are in a state of evolution and construction, and over lifetimes we develop them to the extent that we can step pure Divine, cosmic fire down into our own body without any problem.

Jesus and other great Avatars were able to hold Divine consciousness almost permanently. Avatars and Gurus are strong enough spiritually speaking, to download huge amounts of Divine energy. They then pre-digest it within their own energy system, and download it to us in a manner that we can handle. Thus, the Guru is a living transmission device for energy from the Divine dimension. They can bring it to you before you are capable of bringing it in directly for yourself. They can actually speed up your spiritual evolution with just the touch of a hand. Your spiritual progress will be easier and more rapid because they ignite your spirit, just as one lit candle can light many other candles.

There are always people on earth who can do this. In response to myriad prayers for help, God sends highly developed souls to become people on Earth who are born (or become) conscious channels for Monadic awareness. God can use a physical vehicle (a person) as a channel to get Divine help and love to those who have asked for it.

These Spiritual Olympians exist in every Age, and are like rare pearls. If you study with such people, you will receive deep insights into the nature of reality, and into yourself.

Each conscious and activated Guru is here as an embodiment of Divine love, yet each comes to Earth with a different mission.

Two Gurus with whom I am familiar are Master Choa Kok Sui and Sai Baba. Both are one with their Divine nature. Both of them are priceless souls, and both of them are making positive change in the world. Both of them have strong service mentalities, yet the way they carry out their missions is different.

Sai Baba[8] works as a teacher and also with severely disadvantaged people in India and elsewhere. He founded both general and super specialty

---

[8] There are countless books on the life and work of Sai Baba and it is worth reading the accounts of people whose lives have been miraculously healed by His loving energy.

hospitals in India where treatment is free. He has built water treatment plants throughout his state, and established over three hundred schools and many orphanages. The Sai feeding program takes food to remote villages to many parts of the Indian countryside.

Millions of people have had their lives dramatically improved by Sai Baba's work, vision and mission. His spiritual teachings fill countless books, and nearly every day he sits with people both in massive and intimate groups, teaching and healing, urging people to be the most they can be. He only sleeps a couple of hours per night because he is constantly in a meditative state, charged up by Divine awareness. Miracles of a personal nature have been experienced and documented by countless devotees who seek his guidance.

Master Choa founded Pranic Healing, which is a world-wide school that teaches people how to heal using energy in a very rapid way. Master Choa travels the world over 300 days per year bringing his grace to those who seek it. He is an inspiring and powerful teacher and has millions of students around the world. I once heard his disciples trying to dissuade him from travelling to Cuba, where there was civil unrest going on. He would not listen to them, saying that there were hundreds of souls who were waiting for his blessing. He went to Cuba, endured difficult circumstances, blessed and taught, and left unharmed.

Gurus vary in personality and the way in which they express Divine truths. This happens because they have individual etheric and astral and physical bodies. They live in different cultures in different times and have different jobs to do.

Because part of their consciousness is still human or astral, there is always room for human reactions. If we sit around and wait for them to make some kind of mistake, like being impatient with someone, then we can find evidence of their supposed 'imperfection'. However, their success rate is infinitely better than average. They are first class honours students in how to live, and they embed their Divine wisdom into the culture as it stands now, not as it stood thousands of years ago.

If you are thinking of studying with a Guru, look closely at the people around him or her, at the degree of loving kindness, compassion and understanding inherent in their teachings. Look at the way in which service is part of the philosophy of the teacher, as part of the overall package of how to live properly. As Jesus said, "you can tell a tree by its fruit".

The more we love and honour Gurus for their amazing achievements, the more their considerable grace will flow to us. What the true Guru is, and what they are capable of transmitting, is priceless. They can take you beyond your mind, and propel you into bliss and Divine understanding, provided you are ready, willing and receptive.

The link with a Divine Avatar or Guru is one that forms through the heart, through love and respect. I have studied with five separate Gurus, all of whom have had in common the ability to rapidly expand my consciousness. The message that they bring is always the same: God is love. The way the message comes from Guru to Guru is always different, as a result of their physical, mental, emotional and souls being different. Many colours and flavours of understanding exist, and our job is to find the one that feels comfortable and inspirational, which engenders love, Divine awareness, and healthy, peaceful living. We are so lucky to exist in a time of history where we have great choice and such an amount of Divine help[9].

> *God Is*
> *Sat Chit Ananda*
> *Truth Consciousness Bliss*

---

[9] Just because a spiritual teacher has a lot of students, does not necessarily mean that he or she is a clear channel for Divine energy. If their message is full of judgement and criticism, or desire for revenge, if it says there is only one path to God (theirs) or encourages violence for any purpose, then they are not true embodiments of Divine love, no matter what they may claim to be. As with any spiritual teaching, if it does not resonate with your heart, don't believe it.

Chapter 6

The Soul Dimension

Our soul is a huge, intelligent being that is much larger than our physical body. The soul dimension has more limitations than the Divine dimension. For instance, there is your soul and my soul. There is some degree of separateness here.

The physical, etheric and astral bodies are all a part of our soul, like fingers thumbs and hands are part of our arm. We are really souls not humans. We are just here on Earth having human holidays.

Earth

Our souls exist in the soul dimension through all space and time. Souls grow in wisdom, love, courage, strength and understanding through our experiences over many lives on Earth, and in other places.

The soul dimension is home, and when we are able to connect with this in a conscious way, our whole outlook changes. Life becomes a huge revelation.

Turning Into a Person

Creating humans involved the creation, firstly, of a 'monad'. A monad is the Divine spark within us, paradoxically separate and part of the oneness at the same time. At this level of awareness, we are built in the likeness of God. Each person has a Divine spark inside of them, and this Divine spark, which is really part of the Divine dimension, gives birth to our soul.

What Happens Next

Through the grace of God, the soul is able to decide on its own development, and sets in motion energies and combinations of relationships, and timings for events, which will most effectively create the type of development that the soul desires.

The soul creates a vehicle for itself, which we know as a physical body. It does this by projecting a part of itself down into the physical realm. In order to understand this, think of a great big jug pouring liquid into a cup. The big jug is like the soul, way up in the soul dimension. It is pouring a glass of its contents into the cup, which signifies the physical body. The contents are the Divine and Soul essence, and the stream is the antakarana, or silver cord which always joins us to the greater part of who we are.

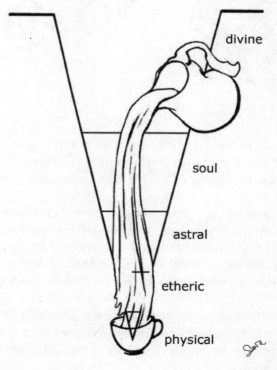

Our souls are genderless, and we incarnate as a man or woman depending on which will suit the purpose of the soul at the time. This makes sexual discrimination pretty silly, because if you are a man you have been a woman before, and vice versa. Racial discrimination is also ridiculous when you consider we incarnate all over the world, in all kinds of cultures through our many lives.

The soul is the major support structure for your body. It is the 'me' that has an existence. It gets into the physical body, in a similar way to how my physical self would get into a car. It is a useful vehicle. When the car wears out, I can trade it in for another one. So it is with the soul and bodies. We incarnate again and again, evolving the extent to which we become aware, until eventually we expand our awareness and wisdom into the fullness of Divine Oneness. This occurs as our etheric bodies get big enough to allow entry by more and more soul presence, and our astral bodies get clear enough not to distort and derail the whole process.

Dying

When we incarnate by being born, we 'die' to the larger understanding of who and what we are. The vast awareness of the Soul is crammed at birth into the small astral consciousness of a little tiny baby person. No wonder they cry!

The soul is our essence, it contains our aliveness, and when the soul leaves the body we are dead. If you have ever had the experience of witnessing someone die, you will understand that one minute there is a person, and the next minute there is not a person, just a husk. There is no essence left. The physical body is definitely not who we are, when you look at it from this perspective.

When we 'die', in terms of the V diagram, we actually just lose our tip. The physical body dies, but the soul and our other bodies do not. The soul extracts information and energy from our astral and etheric bodies and recycles it.

The extracted information is placed within the etheric body of the next baby we become[10]. We do not remember it, because it all happens at a vibrational level that is way off the Richter scale of our awareness, far too high for a normal physical brain to comprehend (and, let's face it, when you are dead, your brain is not much use anyway).

When it extends a part of itself into the denser dimensions (astral and physical), the soul partially loses control of its vehicle. The effects of the astral dimension, the seduction of physical pleasure and security (and what people will do to achieve it), and etheric factors all create extensive challenges. The soul faces many obstacles and tests, and the incarnated part usually can't remember any of this. So here we find ourselves, having a hard time being buffeted around by the challenges of life, seemingly random circumstances, other people, and luck (or lack of it). Fears, confusion and negative beliefs can divert us into endless possibilities of unhappiness, anxiety, and suffering. Life on Earth, which is so taxing on the etheric, astral and physical bodies, provides the soul with many experiences which are formative of its own eventual mature perfection.

Souls exist in different states of maturity, like humans do. There are some that are more experienced and mature than others. Mature souls are more likely to exhibit awareness, kindness, compassion, empathy, courage, tenacity, harmlessness and humour than immature souls will. On the whole, young souls like young children have lots to learn. They might be very cute in their own way, but you don't want to marry one of them!

Heavens - I've turned multidimensional!

---

[10] For more information about this process, see *Meditations for Soul Realization* by Master Choa Kok Sui.

Yes, but why?

The purpose of the incarnation of the soul is to put theory into practice. We are here to learn to master Divine attributes through life on the physical plane. When this happens our astral and etheric bodies become fully infused with soul consciousness. Our chakras become large and filled with golden light. Our thoughts and beliefs are transformed and refined, filled with shanti (peace), prema (love) and ananda (bliss). We are without judgment, and without fear. The perfection of all that is, is understood.

When this occurs, the soul is developed. The incarnated mature soul has far greater capacity for love, intelligence, awareness and understanding of life, and has a much greater sense of empowerment than the average person. They understand universal laws, and are able to use them to create wonderful things on earth for themselves and others.

A person who has managed to wed the physical, astral and etheric vehicles with soul consciousness, is known as a Buddha or one who has achieved Christ consciousness. Another way of saying this is that Shiva (Divine Father) has joined with Shakti (Divine Mother, our human form) and produced a Christed being. This is the ultimate purpose in life. When this happens, we become one with Divine consciousness, and the wheel of rebirth ends.

Great company

The task of spiritual development and becoming Christed is usually very difficult to achieve, so we are given help. As well as physically incarnated Avatars and Gurus, great Beings like angels, Ascended Masters and Holy Teachers exist in the soul dimension. They are here to assist and serve humanity, and to help us evolve and grow. They help us to be inspired and uplifted, and can help show us the way when we tune into them. Beings like Buddha, Quan Yin, Jesus, Mother Mary, Krishna and many others no longer have physical bodies, while they continue to have souls.

Their souls are huge, magnificent, radiant, developed and refined by their previous incarnations, and the level of mastery they achieved during those lifetimes. They are infinitely loving and empowered, through their oneness with God and awareness of their own divinity. Their joy is to see us learn, experience and grow great soul attributes such as love, compassion, tolerance, patience, tenacity, self respect, awareness, inner beauty, forgiveness, inner strength and so on. They, like God, love us unconditionally. They love us even if we don't like them, or don't respect them. They love us when we get things 'right' or when we get things 'wrong.' They do not give up on us. They allow us our own processes and completely respect us and our choices, all of the time. When we pray to them for help they hear us, and energy is immediately sent our way. A lot of their help happens invisibly, but it is possible to learn to have conscious connection to these Great Ones.

Ascended Masters, Holy Teachers and Angels can extend their consciousness and make themselves understood by us on Earth telepathically, through the Astral dimension. This, however, is where problems can start.

Chinese Whispers

The Astral Dimension is usually such a mess that often, what a Soul Dimension Being says is distorted by astral interference, like a children's game of Chinese whispers[11]. What leaves their 'lips' (they don't of course actually have lips) is often very different to that which reaches the mind of the human receiver. Whether the assistance is coming straight from your mighty Higher Soul, or from your loving team of guides, we can get better at receiving that wisdom. To do this, there are several kinds of preparation we can do. A lot of it has to do with cleaning ourselves up, astrally and etherically speaking.

---

[11] In Chinese Whispers, children sit in a circle and one person whispers a message into the ear of the child next to them. That child whispers the same thing to the next child, and so on around the room. Invariably the message is distorted beyond all recognition by the time it comes back to the original source of the message.

Divine Message Distortion

The etheric body is like the soul consciousness receiving hardware. Just say that someone has developed their etheric hardware being the heart, crown and antakarana, to a substantial degree. They are able to bring in from outside of their physical body and mind, information in the form of love and energy. They have a connection to their soul. However, if their astral landscape is still full of garbage, then the information coming from the soul might be distorted. It will be distorted by their own judgments, idiosyncrasies and beliefs.

For instance, a person who has etherically achieved soul connection but has still not mastered judgment and control issues, may interpret the subtle information coming from their soul in a way that fits with their own judgmental ideas. It is not coming purely from love, peace or bliss.

A Natural High

In the astral and physical dimensions there are positive and negative things, like happiness and sadness, sickness and health, and so on. There is no such duality in the soul dimension. Contact with this plane brings with it the Divine attributes of love, joy, happiness and peace. At this level, these feelings are our natural state. The more you cultivate soul consciousness, the better you are ultimately going to feel.

Timeless Vast Intelligence

The soul is not bound by space or time. It has an enormous overview of life, including awareness of things of which our physical consciousness has no idea.

The soul holds the records of our past incarnations. In past life recall, all kinds of events and issues can appear which explain a lot about our fears, phobias, likes and dislikes. When we engage in processes designed to bring soul consciousness, we can get glimpses, and eventually a full picture, of what we experienced before we entered the current physical body that we inhabit.

Conscious union with our Higher Soul brings access to endless wisdom, the ability to be telepathically connected with our guides and spiritual teachers, a heightened sense of intuition and a vastly more pleasant life.

Turning into a Saint, Yogi, Buddha

When we are clear and strong, the higher soul can merge with the incarnated part of itself (the physical, etheric and astral self) fully and completely, creating a new breed of human. Jesus was one such person, a true son of God.

Buddha was another, as was Krishna. There are people like this incarnated now, but there are not many compared to the number of humans. Some are known to the public. Many do not seek interaction with the rest of the world, but serve humanity behind the scenes.

When we become like them, the soul (also known as the 'I AM' presence) is fully developed through all bodies, is one with the Divine consciousness, and has many expanded choices as to what it can do.

Those who have found Divine Oneness can do things that the rest of us would regard as miracles, such as healing the sick, bringing people back from the dead, casting out spirits, creating things in the blink of an eye, assisting others in their evolutionary journey, living in peace, helping people feel love, and so on.

If you look through historical records you can find documentary evidence about the lives of saints. The histories are filled with accounts of miraculous occurrences, including the ability to be in two or more places at once. Time and space do not exist in the soul dimension. If someone has their consciousness present in the soul and Divine dimensions, they are not bound by time or space either. Whether you look at a Christian, Hindu or any other kind of Holy person, bilocation is a common trait of the spiritually advanced, Divinely aware soul.

If you want to read more about saints and yogis and their extraordinary lives, read *Autobiography of a Yogi*, by Paramahansa Yogananda. Yogananda, a great world teacher, left his body in 1952 after bringing the science of yoga to America. He established the Self Realization Fellowship, and his centres are still operating. He helped millions of people find their own Divine essence.

Yogananda was a living saint. His soul had become one with his etheric and astral body. When he died, his body did not decay as bodies usually do. Mr Harry T Rowe, Los Angeles Mortuary director, was responsible for caring for the body of Yogananda prior to his burial. He sent a letter to the Self Realization Fellowship which said:

"The absence of any visual signs of decay in the dead body of Paramahansa Yogananda offers the most extraordinary case in our experience... No physical disintegration was visible in his body even twenty days after death... No indication of mould was visible on his skin, and no visible desiccation (drying up) took place in the bodily tissues. This state of perfect preservation of a body is, so far as we know from mortuary annals, an unparalleled one...No odour of decay emanated from his body at any time... The physical appearance of Yogananda on March 27th, ... was the same as it had been on March 7th the night of his death."

- Autobiography of a Yogi, page 573.

As a matter of normal physical laws, this is impossible. Nevertheless an independent and objective expert, Mr Rowe, confirmed this reality. This is an example of how the physical laws of nature are subject to a higher Divine law, which we contact and activate through our soul development.

Just popping in to help?

When someone has full soul connection, by which their Higher Soul can fully merge with their astral, etheric and physical selves, they may or may not reincarnate again on Earth. They are free of what Buddhists would call the 'wheel of karma', and can stay in a state of grace. Many such perfected beings choose to help their fellow man even though they have no karmic obligation to do so. The Dalai Lama for instance, keeps coming back. As a young child he was able to identify objects he owned in his last life, and this was verified by his former disciples, some of whom the young boy was able to name. He is here to serve humanity, and his grace is evident in his overwhelmingly peaceful and loving presence.

Those perfected individuals who stay around in service to humanity when they could be elsewhere are called 'bodhisattvas'. Sometimes they stay in a physical body like the Dalai Lama, and sometimes they do not take another physical body. They guide their followers by their strong soul and perfected astral vehicles. Mother Mary and Jesus are examples here. Lots of people say they have seen Mother Mary, she appears to those who love her and who need help. This is not unusual for a bodhisattva.

Invisible Biscuits

Enlightened (Divine realized) beings exist in every age. If you have really good karma and sufficient interest, you can find and learn from them. There is less message distortion from a living teacher, because the Divine messages are brought in clearly from the teacher and given to you 'pre-digested' so to speak. People with soul connection know a lot more about their fellow man than others do, simply because they are aware of so much more.

Ram Dass tells an amusing story about an interlude with his teacher. He had been fasting under the direction of the Guru for some months, and then he had to go into town to run some errands. While in town he was unable to resist going to a café and eating some biscuits, which were not on his fasting diet. No one he knew witnessed this little innocent pleasure. When he came back to the Ashram and to his teacher, the first thing the Guru said was, "Did you enjoy the biscuits?" He could see them in the astral body of his student!

Real Estate Advice from Jesus

At one point in my life where I needed guidance, I had a visitation from Jesus. It wasn't in a meditation, but in full waking consciousness. I was waiting outside to collect my son from the babysitter's house, which was across the road from a beautiful lake. The baby sitter was out and I had arrived early. I was thinking about some issues in my life, and wanting some help. I glanced up at the lake and saw Jesus walking over it towards me, smiling. He gazed into my eyes and talked to me for several minutes before he disappeared. The advice he gave me helped me with an immediate problem and created a long term blessing.

This shows that we can get help with anything, even something which in the overall scheme of things, is relatively trivial, such as advice about real estate.

When this event occurred I lived in Cooranbong, a beautiful village north of Sydney. I had moved there to marry my second husband, and I had been in some turmoil about leaving Sydney, where I had lived for a long time and was very happy. To keep my foot in the door, I kept a house in Sydney which I leased to two wonderful young women, Mandy and Kate. I had been on a spiritual path for years by this time, but lately I had been feeling disconnected, confused, and not clear about anything. I had been praying for help. Even so, I did not expect Jesus to come and help me, or to give me such practical advice. He suggested that it would be a good idea to sell the house in Sydney. He did not say why, just that I had asked for guidance and here it was, it was up to me what I did about it. The feeling of love was intense, and even though it was such a strong experience and very visual using ordinary eyesight, I did have a passing thought that I was going crazy.

I am ashamed to say that I did nothing about this conversation. I really did not want to sell the house in Sydney. What would I say to my tenants? What if I wanted to buy back into the market later? The way Sydney prices were rocketing upwards, I might not be able to afford a house in such a nice neighbourhood again. Several weeks passed, and I continued to feel gloomy. By this time I had convinced myself that I had not really spoken to Jesus at all. That is, until it happened again.

Once more I found myself waiting outside the babysitter's house looking at the lake. I was still confused, and still waiting for a bolt from the blue to tell me what to do. Again Jesus walked towards me. I felt overwhelmed. As if in answer to my thought, he said, *"I have given you advice. It could not get any clearer. The rest is up to you."* A feeling of concern for my tenants went through my mind and he said to me, *"Don't you think we have taken care of that?"* Again he smiled at me, and this time it was impossible to pretend that this was not really happening. I resolved instantly to sell the house.

I rang the agent who had sold my last property, and told her to list the house. There was silence over the phone and then the agent Helen said to me: "I have a couple sitting here in front of me who are looking for the exact kind of property that you want to sell. How much do you want for it?" I told her, and she said, "I think you will have yourself a deal. When can we inspect it?" I explained that I had not yet told my tenants, and asked her to wait while I did that. She said she would get them to drive past the house.

Then I faced the difficult task of telling my tenants that they would have to move. I knew they were happy in the house and we had a very good relationship. This was tough. I called and Mandy answered the phone. I told her I was selling and she said "What a relief, Dad has bought us a house and we were moving anyway, we just didn't know how to tell you". Thank you Jesus!

I rang the agent back, and said she could take them to the house right away. She did, they loved it, they paid my price and the house sold that day. No advertising expenses, no fuss.

After that transaction had been exchanged, I found out that a neighbouring farm that I loved in Cooranbong was for sale. I used the money from the Sydney house to purchase the farm, which became the Harmony Centre, a place where thousands of people have connected to a deeper Divine understanding.

Car crash rescue

Sathya Sai Baba, who is embodied presently in India, is able to bilocate and appear at the side of his disciples when they need him. His previous incarnation was as the great Indian saint Shirdi Sai Baba, who was, and still is, loved by millions.

A businessman, Isaac Tigred, who owned a multinational string of coffee shops called Hard Rock Café, is a disciple of Sai Baba's. He tells of many instances where Sai Baba came to his rescue and helped him through difficult, even life threatening situations.

One very graphic story was about how one night he had been driving home from a party totally inebriated. He knew he shouldn't get behind the wheel of his Porsche, but with that much alcohol on board, 'It'll be right" won out over "I should be careful and not drive".

As he drove at ninety miles an hour through twisting mountain roads, he took a bend too fast and careered straight off the side of a mountain. In panic he called out to Sai Baba as he left the road, and the next instant, Sai Baba was sitting beside him in the car, and put his arms across Isaac's body to protect him. The car landed and rolled many times. It was totally destroyed, with wreckage strewn over a large area. Isaac should have been dead, but apart from a few bruises, he was unhurt. Sai Baba, through the faith of his disciple, had created a miracle.

Every day miracles

While every example of help from the higher realms is not necessarily that graphic, higher guidance is a constant source of wisdom, love and guidance. The more you can open to the consciousness of life as your own higher soul views things, the less confusing life becomes. Events that used to seem crazy or unfair, make perfect sense. Cycles make sense. We are surrounded with help, and multi-dimensional laws provide solutions to the endless array of issues that we face in our 'physical' lives.

Following our guidance has a tendency to help us to grow. It pulls us out of ruts and dead ends, and helps us to extend ourselves. Sometimes following our guidance can take courage. So long as our soul connection is strong, and we retain our faith in the Divine, we will always be shown the way forward.

The Soul's Many Lives

Cats might have nine lives, but souls have thousands of them. If we just look at our current life in isolation, there is much that is impossible to understand. However, if we examine our life as part of a continuum of experience, we would see that there is a great deal of sense in everything that happens to us. Much of this has to do with the operation of one of the great laws of our universe, the law of Karma.

Karma is a law that exists regardless of our belief in it. Thus it is not an astral concept (beliefs alter things in the astral world), it is a soul dimension law.

The Law of Karma

When bad things happen it is natural to feel that it isn't fair, why has this happened to me? Why do bad things happen to good people? As a child I used to wonder how God could allow all the pain and injustices in the world to occur. It didn't seem fair. Having since discovered the concepts of reincarnation and karma, it all makes a lot more sense.

Karma is the spiritual law of cause and effect. Every action causes an equal and opposite reaction. The reaction might not happen in the same lifetime.

Jesus taught that those who live by the sword will die by the sword. This is a teaching based on karma. It is also a teaching that is obviously untrue if you look only at one lifetime. Not everyone who lives by the sword dies by it in the same life. However, if you look at a few of their lives in sequence, you can see all of the times they have died by the sword.

My belief is that if something bad happens to me, then it is because I caused something bad to happen to another person in this or another lifetime. Thus, I have to experience the consequences of my actions. Either the exact same thing will happen to me, or I will contract a disease or disability of the same energetic nature.

If a person is born with a terrible health challenge, then there are probably past life events which have karmically necessitated this type of infliction.

At times during healing sessions, people have come face to face with perpetrators of violent and ugly incidents in this life. They have then travelled to another time and place and seen the rest of the story, how they themselves have treated the perpetrator in the past when the tables were turned and the perpetrator was the victim of the client. Having witnessed this, they are then guided through a forgiveness exercise, by which they can ask for forgiveness from all the people that they have hurt in this or any other lifetime. Then they are often able to make the decision to forgive those who have hurt them in this life.

The law of karma cannot be trifled with, but it can be affected by the operation of a higher law, which is the 'law of forgiveness'. Jesus was the ultimate teacher of this law. He said that it is a good idea to practise forgiveness, or to 'turn the other cheek'.

This is much harder to do than to feel rage, vengeance and intense emotional pain. Some people become defined by their tragedies, and hang onto them as though there is no other alternative. Even suggesting that they might try to forgive the person who has hurt them, causes an angry and accusatory reaction. This means that the issue is still energetically alive inside them, and will continue to cause suffering until it is healed through forgiveness.

When grief and grudges are held in the heart, we are the ones that suffer. While it is easy to find ourselves in conflict situations where we are at odds with other people, the journey of life is about finding ways to forgive whatever has happened, allowing the heart to operate fully again. Grief, grudges and animosity cut us off from the natural flow of love and bind us to the people concerned. We are tied together through an uncomfortable cord of co-dependence, attachment and pain.

It is natural to feel anger, grief, denial, and lots of painful emotions when we are hurt by the actions of another person. It can take time to come to terms with it. Sometimes this is really difficult to do, especially if we feel that we are victims to something over which we had no control.

Without wishing to underestimate the emotional pain that these types of events cause, we do in the end have a choice as to how we deal with it.

If we identify with our history of hardship year in year out, then it lives continually in our consciousness, and everything is affected by it. The darkness stays with us. In this way, we can become very stuck. We can cut ourselves off from many of the pleasures and possibilities that life has to offer, because we cannot get over the event or the people who hurt us. Our identification is bound up in our position as a victim to the past. All of this heavy energy shrinks the heart chakra and makes soul connection very difficult.

Creating problems

When we are attacked by another person either verbally or physically, it can be really difficult not to feel like a victim. From a physical perspective, clearly 'they' have just done something that is inappropriate. If we expand our awareness and look further however, we will see that the reason for this event will exist in a perfect balance of fairness. There is a definite temptation in these situations to sit in judgment of an attacker and hold the moral high ground, blaming the other person for the issue. This way, the victim can hold themselves right and all wrongdoing can be externalized and seen only in the other person. This might feel good, but it is not helpful, because it will serve to disempower the victim. They will forever be at the mercy of others, buffeted around by the folly of their fellow man.

The soul carries a burden of karma, which plays out in our physical life like a big drama.

JOANNA
Joanna was a chartered accountant working for one of the leading firms in Sydney. She was good at her job, and had recently been made a partner. She had budget targets to meet, and when I met her for a healing she was stressed, anxious, not centered and not meeting her budgets. Further, she was being harassed at work by a powerful senior female partner we will call Fiona, who took every opportunity to make her life miserable. Fiona criticized her and undermined her with other members of the firm. This treatment had started

the minute Joanna walked in the door and had been relentless. She had no idea what had caused this instant reaction in the senior woman, or what she had done or failed to do that had offended her. She felt completely victimized and wronged.

I talked to Joanna about the issue of karma, and how sometimes unresolved issues between souls from one lifetime, leak into the current lifetime. Soul family travels through time and space with us, assuming different roles as we do, so as to bring each other to the full fruition of our potential as Divine human beings.

As soon as I looked in her crown chakra, I saw Joanna as a Maori woman who was the wife of the Chief. Her son had chosen to marry a girl from another tribe, much to the annoyance of Joanna in that life. Joanna (who was not Joanna then, but the same soul) made this woman's life hell. She failed to show her any warmth and excluded her from all kinds of women's activities. Her daughter-in-law could do nothing to please her and was miserable, angry and confused. In this life the daughter-in-law had incarnated as Fiona. The tables were turned and this time it was Fiona who was the matriarch of a 'tribe' (the firm) and Joanna was the junior newcomer. What she was experiencing was the flip side of the treatment she had handed out all those years ago in a completely different lifetime with the same soul.

I helped Joanna through a forgiveness exercise, and cut all of the cords of energy that were binding them together. I asked that because Joanna had learned from the experience and developed more compassion, that the situation be healed. Joanna was asked to send love to Fiona whenever she meditated over the coming weeks, to complete the healing.

A few weeks later Joanna rang me and told me that the healing had been miraculous. Instead of picking on her, Fiona was now friendly and encouraging. At a company dinner, Fiona made a speech about what a good job Joanna had done on a particular project.

Instead of remaining in victim consciousness, Joanna had done something about the situation. She had accepted responsibility for what was happening in her life. Through this act of self empowerment, she had been able to access the karmic release of the situation and bring peace to her life.

Not Fatalistic

Interestingly, the law of karma is not fatalistic and will bend and accommodate you in certain circumstances. When you forgive someone, the heavy energy attachment which shrinks the heart chakra disappears, and is replaced by a vibrant energy of love and acceptance. This is a key to the development of higher consciousness.

Good Service

Several years ago I was traveling from Sydney to our farm, to collect our skis and take the kids on a holiday in the snow. I was driving north on a freeway which was partly cut through the surrounding hills, with exposed sandstone rock faces on either side of the road. It was pouring with rain, and the heavy traffic was moving slower than usual. We rounded a bend and descended a steep hill through a cut out section of the mountain. Off the side of the road were a number of vehicles which had been involved in a collision earlier that day. The car in front of me braked suddenly, presumably to see what was happening. I was driving a big heavy four wheel drive vehicle, and was unable to stop. When I hit the brakes, my car aquaplaned on the wet road and I lost control. The car drove front on into the sandstone wall at the side of the road and all I could hear was my daughter Rachel screaming. I remained conscious despite the heavy impact, and remember fearing that the cars behind me would crash into our car, which had skidded at right angles blocking the entire roadway.

Somehow, the cars behind us managed to stop and not hit our vehicle. Apart from being really shaken up, Rachel was unharmed. The emergency workers walked over to our car and forced open my door, and said, "Good morning can we help you?" They asked our names and helped us out of the car, at which time I noticed that I was unable to walk on my right leg. The dashboard of the car had been pushed inwards and had rammed into my knee and chipped a bone. Rachel and I were helped into the back of a fire truck out of the rain, and the tow truck and police instantly took care of my car which was written off.

Rachel was slightly in shock, and we needed some oxygen for her. Unfortunately there was no ambulance present, as the people in the previous accident had been taken away in it. The man in the car behind me came over and said "I am an off duty ambulance driver on my way to work, can I assist you?" He then cared for Rachel and I until the ambulance came to us.

By this time my neck was hurting and my fingers were going numb. So I was strapped to a spinal board in case I had spinal injuries, and taken to a nearby hospital. When we arrived in casualty we were treated immediately. There was no delay in having neck and knee x-rays, and I am relieved to say there was nothing wrong with my neck other than a slight case of whiplash.

My knee remained troublesome and I limped very noticeably. An enlightened teacher Greg came to visit and gave me healing. He told me that the accident was a karmic matter. He said that in a previous incarnation I had been responsible for locking up and imprisoning a lot of people unfairly. So in this life I had been likely to suffer paraplegia or quadriplegia, which is the ultimate form of imprisonment inside your own body. In that accident I had the potential to sustain catastrophic injury, through the operation of the law of cause and effect.

Since I had been a spiritual teacher for several years, had done thousands of healings to alleviate the suffering of others, and had overcome and forgiven some pretty distressing problems and people in my life, I had developed a lot of karmic grace. Grace, or Divine energy of love, can counteract anything, and can soften the harsh effects of our own previous wrongdoings.

On that day I found out first hand how important it is to develop grace, and to ensure that my personal karma had softened. Instead of paraplegia I would have a tricky knee instead. It was not painful, and even the chipped bone and soft tissue damage did not ache or cause any discomfort, although it tended to collapse if I walked on it. Today the effect is minimal. I have never forgotten how relatively graceful the entire experience was, and how it could have redefined my life had I chosen differently in earlier years.

Develop Grace – Multi-dimensional Insurance

One of the primary ways in which we can insure ourselves against calamity is to develop karmic grace. We do this through the hard inner work of forgiveness, being of service to others, and giving. These are three primary methods of insuring ourselves in the multi-dimensional world in which we live.

Whatever we give out will come back. Locking people up, causes us to be locked up as well, or leads us to experience an illness of the same imprisoning vibration. If we engage in malicious gossip, others will gossip about us and cause us harm. Giving sloppy service to others means we will receive sloppy service. If we are dishonest, others will be dishonest to us. Helping others means we will be helped when we need it.

Giving creates the precondition for receiving, and is directly relevant to living a life of abundance and happiness. Forgiving releases the blackness of grief, anger, rage and resentment from your heart. Service allows others to serve you. Each of these three things creates energy of a very high vibration, and cultivates love as well as the heart chakra.

You never know when you might need grace, so start to develop some now. Grace is the wind beneath our wings when we need it. You can avoid disaster that you never knew was coming through giving, forgiving and being of service to others.

Chapter 7

Soul Vibration

The vibration of the soul is incredibly high. In this dimension, there is no negative and positive. There is just love, joy, happiness, peace, wisdom and awareness. We all want to enjoy these states of mind. I doubt that there is anyone on Earth who doesn't.

The only negative and positive experience that is possible where the soul is concerned, is whether we are actually experiencing soul vibration or we are not. When that vibration is present, we feel amazing. All is coated with love. There is deep understanding of astral reality, and amazing connection to our Divine parent. There is also the potential of merging with any other soul-realized being in a loving and happy way.

The feeling of soul union is joyful. When we are first learning to hold that vibration, we fall in and out of it, back and forth between soul and astral vibration. The degree to which this occurs depends on many factors, and everyone will probably have a slightly different experience of this. However, the feeling of full union, which for me occurs when I am teaching or meditating, lasts for some time after the meditation or class finishes. It then slowly resolves and I am aware that I am back in astral consciousness again. Each time I reach into Soul consciousness, the effect is stronger and lasts longer. Eventually I am sure that the merging will be permanent.

Unhappiness, and the entire negative end of the astral range of possibility, only exists because we are not in full soul union. We are in the astral dimension, a learning zone where polarities exist, and we learn through experience, the amazing possibilities of creation.

Through raising our vibration and gradually eliminating negative choices from our repertoire, we slowly float vibrationally upwards in our thoughts, emotions and beliefs (all of which are astral) into a vibration that matches that of the soul. When that happens we can naturally flow into soul connection.

The consciousness of most humans is very astrally based. It is all very well talking about how soul consciousness works, but this is not much use if people are unable to resolve astral blockages. So as to gracefully manage the astral dimension, we need to understand how it functions, as this has a big impact on what it is that we experience in our physical lives. Mastering the astral dimension gives rise to mastery of life on Earth.

Astral fun and games

The workings of our mind and the management of our emotions are largely astral matters. Much of the difficulty we have in life stems from the astral dimension. The astral dimension does not have its own light source, and relies on light from above and below to illuminate it. The astral part of us can also be called the egoic self. It can be so tricky, that many spiritual traditions choose to bypass the astral dimension altogether.

Spiritual aspirants spend their time developing an appeal to God to help them, and God does. There are innumerable ways to find God, but they fall mostly into two distinct camps. We can achieve union with God either through mastery of the astral dimension, or through ignoring it altogether and getting God to come and get us. The following story, told by Sai Baba, graphically illustrates the situation[12].

Big Black Dog

Imagine that God is the occupant of a large two storey house surrounded by a large fence with a gate in it. All you have to do to know God is to come in through the gate and go into the house, up the stairs and there is God. The only problem is that in the yard is a huge ferocious black dog. You know that if you go through that gate, the dog will rip you to pieces. The big black dog is your ego, your astral body. While we are on Earth, the ego separates us from Divine oneness. The yard, which is the distance we have to travel, is the journey of life.

You have two options. One option, used by some spiritual aspirants, is to sing out to God to come and get you. When you do this with enough conviction, God comes and easily controls the dog. The dog respects God and does whatever God says. God accompanies you, and you never really have to deal with the big black dog. All you had to do is sing out loudly.

Another option is that you learn to get on with the big black dog. The big black dog will always be there, and is an inescapable part of reality. Unless you want to sing out to God every time you want to enter His home, you will have to learn to manage the dog.

Since the dog is so huge and ferocious, you cannot fight it. The dog will win. So, you start to love it. The dog feels the love coming from you, and calms down. It comes over for you to pat it. You tell it what a nice doggy it is. It is still as dangerous as ever, but it likes you and won't hurt you. You give

---

[12] Sanathana Sarathi, September 1998, from *Aura of the Divine*, 1999 Sri Sathya Sai Books and Publications Trust, India.

it a bone, and it is happy. You are safely able to walk through the yard into God's house and go upstairs to God. You can come and go as you like. There is so much love (God) inside you that you are in fact one with God. So long as you maintain love in your heart, the black dog can never hurt you and will not scare you.

Whenever you forget about love and instead resonate to judgment, condemnation, criticism, grudges and other negative states of being, you better watch out. The dog will be growling and consuming you. God (love) might have to come and rescue you again, so sing out.

Six of one half dozen of the other

Neither of the approaches exemplified in the big black dog story are more correct than the other, and a lot of the choice comes down to personality factors. The 'straight to God' approach is effective, and is assisted by a great deal of time spent in contemplation. It is suited to those who prefer a monastic approach to life. There is minimal interaction with the 'real' world and the 'big black dogs' of everyone else. Through deep meditation and spiritual practices, the aspirant comes to know God and to anchor a high vibration of energy on Earth, in the region where they live. We need people who do this. However problems can erupt when they interact with others if no work on the ego has been done.

The second method, becoming friends with the big black dog, is more suited to those who chose to remain in the mainstream world while they develop their spiritual connection and Divine awareness. Taking any action and decisions in the world, earning a living, caring for a family and social interaction necessitate astral activity and give rise to a lot of opportunities for learning. There can be quite a lot of scope for conflict both on a large and small scale. Learning how to make friends with the egoic self makes life a lot easier and is a very practical way to make a difference in the world.

Millennia of people singing out to God to come and rescue them has given us some great stories of miraculous events, but looking around at the world, it has not brought us peace. Given that the 'Path of Ease and Grace' is a mainstream spiritual approach for the general population, in my view it is desirable to learn how to make friends with the big black dog. Much of the information in the following pages will help you do this.

For either path you need a healthy etheric body, and then the Royal road paved with Gold will eventually take you through your heart, crown and soul star chakras into Divine union. The difference is, when you return to the world focus, if you are friends with the big black dog you will be less hampered, better equipped and less likely to blame others for any difficulties you face in life.

PART 3
The Etheric Dimension

Chapter 8

The Etheric Dimension

Our etheric body is the body through which the intelligence, love and energy from our soul selves reaches us in the physical world. If the soul energy is electricity, then the etheric body is the supply lines that bring it to our house. The house represents our physical form. If everything in our house runs on 240 volts, things will overload if the huge voltage from the power source is not stepped down to us in some way. For this reason we have a series of transformers (chakras) along the line, turning 33,000 volts down to a useful 240 volts.

We have many chakras above our head that help in this process. By the time the high voltage Divine and soul energy gets to our crown chakra, it is able to be absorbed into our body. Each chakra has a role in the absorption of energy from our soul selves, and when things are working as they are designed to, we are healthy, vital, happy and in tune with the Divine. Sometimes this ideal condition is not the case, and some effort is required to come back into balance.

Our physical self is supported etherically by a whole sea of subtle energy or prana, which pervades our bodies, minds, relationships and the things that we create in our lives. If the flow is interrupted, we feel this as blockages and issues in our life.

My Etheric What?

Your etheric body comprises your aura, your chakras and the meridians through which energy is pumped throughout your being.

Meridians are the lines, somewhat like non-physical nerves, through which stimuli flows from one chakra or energy centre to another.

When we are looking at the etheric body the general rule is, the bigger the better. A really fabulous etheric body is characterized by being clean and bright as well as big. The bigger the etheric body, the more spiritual voltage you can handle.

The Aura

The aura is like a bubble of light energy around you. It can be photographed through kirlean photography, and can be felt with the hand if you know how. It is your personal space.

The various stresses, emotional judgements and limiting thought forms that we carry around with us, can cause the aura to become dull, droopy and clogged up with garbage. We feel rotten, can't think clearly, and our energy is all over the place. When the aura is droopy and dull, full of stress, tension and built-up emotions, you might become unwell, or have little energy, optimism and enthusiasm. People don't tend to find you so appealing.

When the aura is big, bright and bouncy, you appear healthy and well. A healthy aura is full of life, vitality and energy, and attractive to others. When soul infusion starts to become more intense, the size of the aura gets bigger. It becomes more like a force field. When you are in the presence of someone who is in full contact with their higher soul, the strength of their energy can feel like a blissful force coming out of them. Their energy permeates whoever they meet, if they are receptive to the experience.

Chakras

The chakras are spinning vortexes of energy. We have lots of them, all over the body. The most important and powerful chakras are those set out in the drawing below.

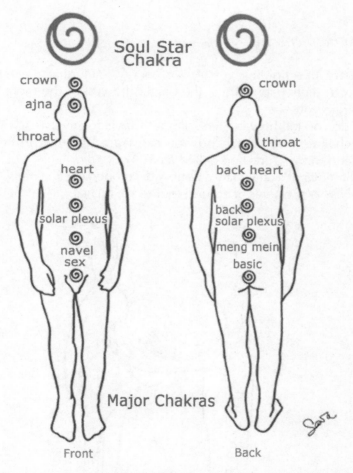

Each of the major chakras has a discrete set of functions that it performs. All of them operate by spinning back and forwards like a washing machine agitator, taking clean energy into our body and expelling dirty energy from our body.

clockwise spins energy in   anticlockwise spins energy out

Cups to hold energy

Chakras are like holding vessels for energy, including the energy sent to you by your higher soul. Thus, the bigger the vessel, the more the soul can download to you.

How do you tell how big a chakra is? That is relatively easy. You can learn to scan chakras with your hand. You can learn scanning in Pranic Healing classes, and in my workshop called *Ignite Your Spirit*.

The diameter of a chakra tells us how developed the chakra is. Most average chakras have a diameter of around four to six inches.

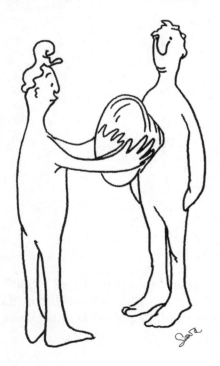

When a chakra is larger than ten inches, it has an ability to handle huge amounts of energy. The person will have sufficient energy, development and power to be a leader, and to walk the world stage in whatever endeavour they choose.

On the other end of the scale, chakras that are undersized may account for localized problems. People who are mentally slow have chakras in the head area which are smaller than normal. People with small sex chakras have low libido, and so on.

We can do exercises to increase the size of our chakras. This is like etheric weight lifting. As with physical weight lifting, we need to do it repetitively for there to be real development.

Our thoughts, values, attitudes and tendencies are held within our chakras, and are brought to our conscious mind through the brain. When you change your chakras, you change the way you think. Not only that, you change your energy, your vibration, your resonance with people places and events, and therefore you change your life.

Ignite Your Spirit

The etheric body is such a big topic that I have written a separate book about it called *Ignite Your Spirit*. It deals with the ins and outs of chakras, and the incredible possibilities inherent within them. Easy exercises to build the chakras are set out in this book.

Etheric development leads to the ability to have greater soul connection, and to have a more balanced, interesting and healthy life. Since the energy centres or chakras are so important in our overall development and to soul connection, some of the information from Ignite Your Spirit has been summarized here for ease of reference.

Accidentally getting messy

Chakras store and organise our values and beliefs. After years of processing immense amounts of information through education, listening to family and the media, and interacting with others, our chakras are charged with the energy and beliefs that reflect what we have fed them. Some of what we have fed them is good and wholesome, and is of a high vibration. It will make the chakra gather strength and flourish. However some of it is pretty toxic and harmful, and is of a low vibration. This can make our chakras wither and slow down.

Stress and other forms of etheric and astral debris can cause our energy centres to become clogged and congested. Stress is a huge problem in

Western society and alarmingly, statistics show it is increasing. There is something wrong. We are not a happy culture and we find it difficult to feel inner peace.

In Australia, one in 10 people take medication to help them sleep, and depression is the second most prevalent condition for which people see a doctor. Hypertension (high blood pressure, also caused largely from stress) is the most common complaint for which Australians see doctors.

Medication to change our consciousness is used not only through medical intervention, but socially. The use of alcohol and drugs to achieve relaxation and happiness would not be necessary if we knew how to achieve the ultimate happiness of soul connection.

Like lint in the filter of a clothes dryer, too much stress forms garbage in a chakra and slows it down. Eventually, if enough garbage builds up, the chakra can stop operating altogether. This means trouble.

No one tries to mess themselves up. It's just that we do not know how not to. Energy healing can undo the mess, but eventually you have to take stock and adjust your life so that you don't keep creating big, energetically costly, imbalances in your life.

Like muscles, you need to use chakras or you slowly lose them. When chakras don't operate efficiently they stagnate and slowly shrink. The normal spinning motion of the chakra, which brings clean energy in and takes dirty energy out, does not happen properly. This leads to a problem of under activation of the chakra: it is too clogged up to function at the right speed and do its job. It is unable to bring the necessary vital energy into the body. Systems close down, and depression or health issues can result.

Depression is the closing down of energy centres in the body. When the base chakra closes down we don't want to live. When the sex chakra shuts down we have no libido. When the navel chakra fails we have digestive problems and feel powerless. When the solar plexus stops functioning we have poor self esteem. When the heart chakra closes down we cannot feel love or inner peace. When the throat chakra shuts down we cannot and don't want to talk to anyone. We lose interest in the detail of our life. When the ajna chakra stops functioning we do not know which way to turn. When the crown chakra closes down we feel despair.

Depression, as it spreads through our chakra system, cuts us off from life, other people, and from happiness, vitality and hope. Medication for depression is often an incomplete solution.

To me depression is a spiritual disease, as well as a medical one. Using soul energy, depression can be quickly reversed in the majority of people. It does not work for everyone, just as not all people are assisted by the various types of medication available to treat the condition. When energy healing does not work to treat depression it is often because the person is not receptive to energy healing, and has pre-judged that it will not work. Thus they block the flow of energy. Others are unable to be assisted because they do not have sufficient karmic grace to be lifted out of their suffering. In the majority of cases however, Ignite Your Spirit healing makes a miraculous and sometimes instantaneous change in a person's wellbeing. They are quickly able to wean themselves from all medication, under the supervision of their doctor. How to use the energy of your soul to Ignite Your Spirit and how to improve your karma, are dealt with later in this book.

JILL

Jill was a senior banker who had a difficult start in life. Her mother was severely depressed, and had attempted suicide many times during Jill's teenage years. Several times Jill had to save her mother, including bandaging her wrists after she had slashed them, and calling the ambulance. Not surprisingly, Jill had developed depression herself and had been plagued by it her whole adult life. She was about to turn 40 and was unable to escape from the grip of the latest severe bout of depression.

Jill attended a soul connection workshop at The Harmony Centre. There happened to be a clinical psychiatric psychologist in the class, who at morning tea had a private word to me. He told me that Jill was displaying signs of morbid depression and advised me to keep an eye on her. It was not hard even for a lay person to see that Jill was in a bad way. Her eyes were glazed and she exuded hopelessness and resignation. It was as if she had given up on life. Jill told me later that she had been feeling suicidal for days.

During the seminar there was a class exercise involving the use of soul energy to clean the chakras and promote wellbeing. This had the effect of lightening Jill's mood a little, but she was still very ill and dejected. The amount of soul energy being used by the people in the class was having a positive effect but it would take a lot of time and treatment to heal her.

Later in the seminar during meditation with the group, I went through a state of soul connection, by which the Guru or monadic consciousness arose within me. I placed my hand on Jill and Divine energy poured into her. She had a healing that took place at a very high voltage. It took less than a minute.

Within hours, all trace of the depression was gone. Her eyes were bright and she was smiling. She went on to complete all of the workshops and to organize workshops for us in various places. Even when her boyfriend ditched her a week later, she was able to deal with it in a positive way. She moved interstate and led a wonderful life.

Her own soul connection formed, and she was intuitively strong. She did not fall into the pit of depression again. From time to time she felt down, and could feel the edges of depression, but through meditation and connection with her spiritual teacher, she was able to avoid returning to her long term problem.

This miracle occurred because Jill had the karmic grace for recovery. She had always been kind and generous, and had a strong service mentality. She was open to the concept of energy healing. Unwittingly she had planted the seeds of her own recovery through her compassionate actions during this and prior incarnations.

Getting back in the groove

If you have been stressed, anxious or depressed, get some energy healing from a reputable healer with whom you feel relaxed, and who radiates wellbeing and happiness.

If a chakra is very under activated, it often only needs a clean to jump back into life again. Energy can flow into it, and it can operate properly again. When all of your chakras are spinning away merrily, you will feel much better than you may have in years.

When all of our chakras are in balance, our life will reflect this. Ideally, all of our major chakras should be the same size as each other[13] and they should all be big, bright and beautiful.

Unfortunately, this is often not the case. Sometimes people have one chakra that is massive compared to the others. At the other extreme, some people have one chakra that is tiny compared to all the others. Whether they are out of balance because they are too big or too small, this can warp our perception. Unbalanced chakras can also cause health problems. If you would like to know about this, refer to the Pranic Healing books by Master Choa Kok Sui.

---

[13] With the exception of the back of the navel chakra, called the meng mein chakra, which should be no more than half the size of the others. If it is bigger than that, there is a risk of high blood pressure.

Chakras and consciousness

For ease of understanding, here are some words which summarize the specialized areas of each major chakra, in terms of our overall consciousness and aptitudes.

Crown chakra — Inspiration, Divine consciousness, soul guidance

Ajna Chakra — Free will, use of will, understanding concepts, the 'big picture' of life

Throat Chakra — Detail, communication, logic, implementation of the big picture, creativity.

Heart Chakra — Love, kindness, compassion, sharing and empathy

Solar Plexus — Self esteem, receiving, putting self first, tenacity, strength and courage, daring, individuality.

Navel Chakra — Personal power, assimilation of energy, speed of reflexes

Sex chakra — Magnetism, creativity, sexuality, birthing.

Base chakra — Security, money, family ties, physical world focus.

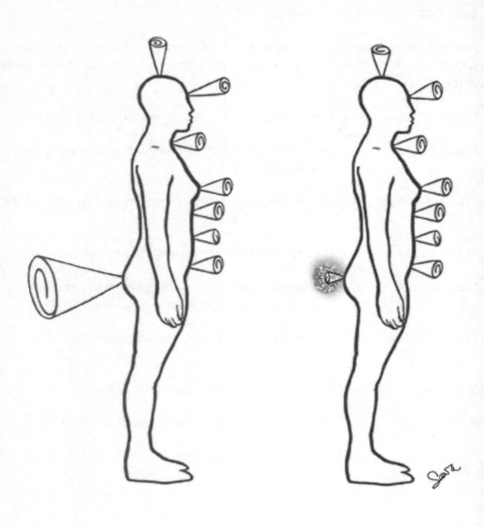

If the base chakra is too big, a person will focus too much on money and security. Someone with a small base chakra, or one that is congested and full of energetic garbage, might not be very grounded or practical. They may also suffer financial challenges, back problems, or have a lot of family dramas.

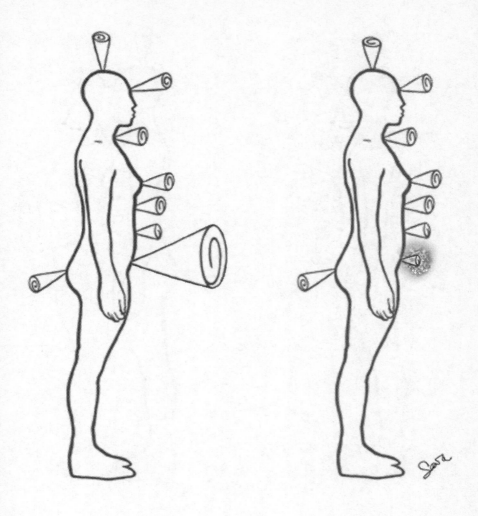

Someone with a big sex chakra will be focused on, well, sex. They can be highly creative and magnetic people. A small sex chakra can mean limited personal magnetism, or not much creative energy. Blocked and congested sex chakras can create menstrual or bladder problems, or poor libido.

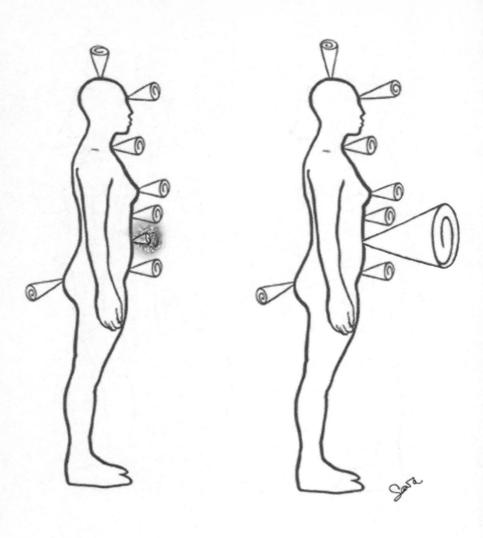

A very big navel chakra will give a natural focus on power. Whether this manifests as power over others, or empowerment *of* others, depends on the balance of other chakras. Those with large navel chakras are often attracted to speed and adrenalin stimulating activities. A very small navel chakra often belongs to someone who is prone to giving away their power. This leads to difficulties in relationships. Congested navel chakras can lead to stomach problems.

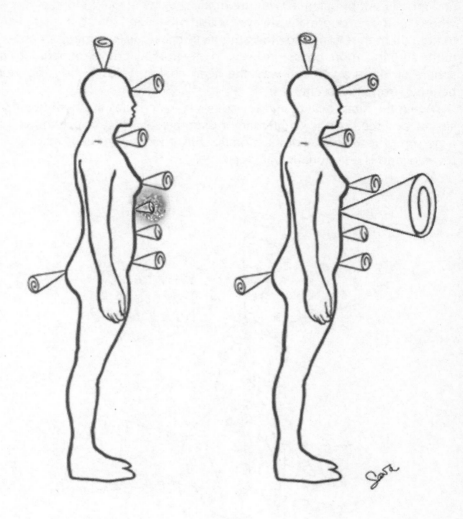

Where a person has a big solar plexus chakra, they are generally self confident and strong. When it is huge and out of proportion to the other chakras, the person can be self obsessed. A really small solar plexus chakra gives rise to self esteem issues. When the solar plexus chakra is congested, it is a rabbit warren of stored negative emotions, and the person is likely to be harbouring a lot of unexpressed anger or even rage. It feels unpleasant to have a solar plexus chakra that is larger than the other chakras, and if it is also congested (full of low vibrational energy) this sometimes causes personality issues such as self-centred behaviour and bullying.

A big heart chakra gives a focus on giving and loving. Someone with a small or congested heart chakra can suffer from emotional shut down, and is not likely to be very empathetic or compassionate. When the heart chakra is huge and grossly out of balance with the other chakras, it can belong to someone who is a bit of a 'doormat', always serving others and never allowing anyone to help them in return. Growth of the heart chakra is essential for connection to the soul in a more conscious way. To integrate that development into every sphere of life in a graceful way, the heart chakra needs to be *supported* by healthy, strong lower chakras.

When the heart chakra and the solar plexus chakras are both healthy and strong, and the heart is slightly larger than the solar plexus chakra, you have a person who is kind, compassionate, has good self esteem, can give and receive, and is emotionally balanced.

A big throat chakra denotes someone who is focused on communicating, or on detail, such as is needed for creating a painting, or setting up logical systems. A person with a small throat chakra can be a poor communicator, and may not be very good at detail. If the throat chakra is far larger than the other chakras, the logical and critical functions in a person can control the system. These people are challenging to be around because nothing is ever good enough, and they want to tell you so, often.

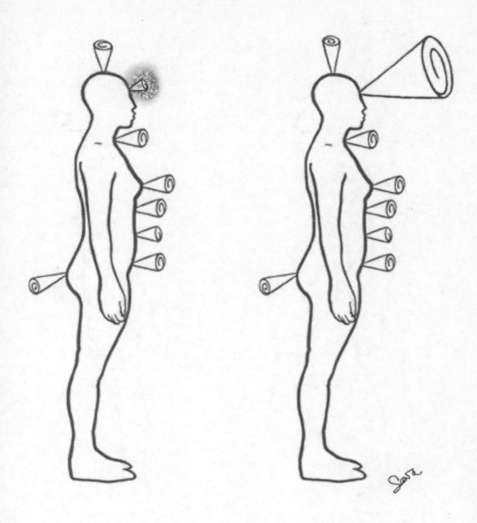

A big ajna chakra usually belongs to someone who is used to being in control and exerting their will. When it is huge and out of balance with the other chakras, the person can be somewhat overbearing. When the ajna is too small, the person may have difficulty exerting their will at all. Thus they may be prone to being pushed around.

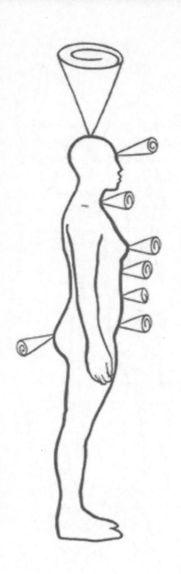
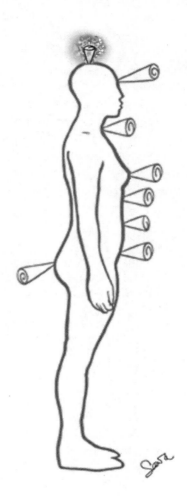

A really huge crown chakra will belong to someone who is focused on spirituality. A very small crown chakra, or a very congested one, will denote a person who is quite closed to Divine reality, not very imaginative and possibly extremely stressed or prone to headaches.

When any of our chakras become either excessively large or disproportionately small, it can warp our perception. One very large chakra will give us expanded consciousness in the particular sphere of life that the chakra looks after, giving us a natural bias or aptitude in the area concerned. One very small chakra will inhibit us in the particular sphere of life which the chakra would normally govern, and give us problems functioning in this area.

Combinations of chakral shapes give rise to different personality dispositions. If the ajna and heart chakras are large, a person will probably be very loving in the way they exercise their strong will. If the ajna and solar plexus are huge but the heart chakra is small, they might be very selfish or egocentric in the way they exercise their will.

Someone with a big throat chakra combined with a big heart chakra will be able to enjoy (and probably make good money from) detailed work. A big heart chakra combined with a big sex chakra can be a very loving and creative person. A large throat chakra combined with a big solar plexus chakra, may give rise to a highly organized and fearless person. When combined with a small or very congested (dirty) solar plexus chakra (which would denote a lack of self esteem) a big throat chakra can be picky and negative, always finding fault with others so that they can feel better about themselves by maintaining the moral high ground.

The shape of things

As a general rule of thumb, those with big lower chakras, and small upper ones, are more attuned to the physical world. They are interested in concrete things. They are geared towards making and having money, and surviving in the physical world. They focus on assets, stability and security. In Western culture, we talk about the importance of the refined and loving values of the upper chakras, but more awareness and emphasis is generally placed on the things controlled by the lower chakras.

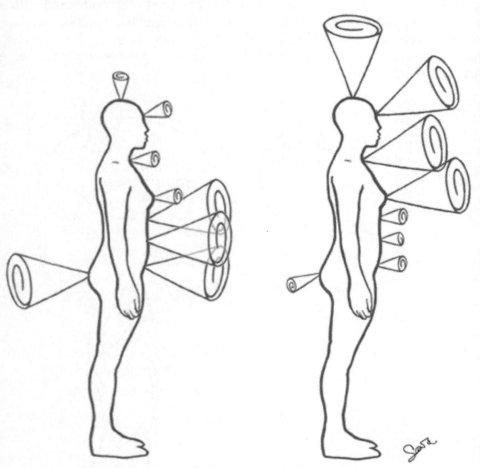

Without upper chakra development, there will be little in the way of loving kindness, sensitivity and appreciation of the inner, spiritual world. People with big lower chakras and small upper chakras do not have the etheric hardware necessary to be able to perceive subtle stimuli flowing from the soul and Divine dimensions, thus they are prone to proclaiming that it does not exist. To them, it doesn't.

Those with big upper chakras have an easier time perceiving subtle energy, and are more likely to be attuned to God and the world of emotions, angels and the like. They have big, spiritual receptors (found in the upper chakras) so they are able to have real and meaningful soul contact.

Without lower chakra development, people with big upper chakras may struggle to flourish in the physical world. They frequently have financial challenges. They can be impractical, suffer from procrastination and lack direction.

The aim is to have big upper chakras AND big lower chakras. Then we can lead a really balanced and spiritually aware life. Just like we can run faster and see more colours than our ancestors, so it is that we are developing stronger, brighter and cleaner energy fields than our predecessors. This will be an important legacy for our children and generations to come. Eventually this kind of science will be taught in schools, and will be just as important as basic biology and language skills.

Chapter 9

Chakras and soul connection

Awareness of our Divine nature is not possible without a certain degree of etheric development in the upper energy centres, particularly in the heart and crown chakras. Someone with a big heart and crown chakra is naturally attuned to the reality of the soul and Divine world.

Becoming a Golden Being

As our soul awareness develops, the degree and quality of energy that fills our being changes. Instead of the ordinary energy we get from the sun, food, water and air, your chakras can become golden and filled with Divine energy. When viewed clairvoyantly, a person who is filled with the energy of their higher soul looks golden. They glow. A person with large golden chakras and a large golden aura feels good to be around, and will uplift you with their radiant soul energy.

In this painting of Jesus, notice the halo around Him. In the original painting the halo is golden, as is his sacred heart. He was totally infused with the energy of his soul, and thus he was able to anchor his monadic or Divine self. He became totally Christed, a true son of God. He was connected to all that is. This is a rare example of what is achieved at the pinnacle of human development.

The voltage of energy and power that can shine through a Christed person is much greater than average. They can do things that a normal 240 volt person cannot do. They not only feed their own being, but are radiant forces that energetically feed all who seek a closer Divine connection, in a spirit of love.

By developing our chakral system, we can safely allow more and more soul and Divine energy into our being, which will in turn expand our consciousness. We will become wiser and more loving. This allows for a graceful transformation through which all of us, in time, can become Christed.

A triplicity of Chakras: Heart, Crown and Soul

The heart and the crown are the main chakras that are relevant to soul connection. In time a third chakra, our soul star chakra, also becomes active and a part of our conscious evolution.

Heart Chakra

The heart chakra in the middle of the chest, and the crown chakra on the top of the head, are the entry points for Divine energy and inspiration. They are the doorway to your relationship with your Divine parent.

Crowning Glory

The crown chakra has been known about for eons. Clairvoyantly those with large crown chakras look like they are wearing golden jewelled headdresses. It is the development in their energy anatomy that makes them look that way.

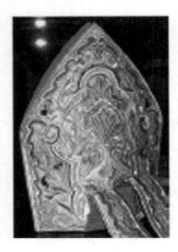

The hats worn by various clergy are usually golden or jewelled, and resemble crowns or mitres. Here is a picture of a cardinal's mitre. It was originally meant to signify the crown chakral development of the wearer.

Prayer and meditation assist in the development of the crown chakra. When the crown chakra is sufficiently large and clean, we attain vastly expanded perceptions because we are able to go beyond our finite mind more easily. We enter into unity consciousness, and can *download* information that we have never actually studied.

One of the things we can do at this level of development is gain access to the 'akashic records'. These records contain every single thing that has occurred in every lifetime that we have experienced. Past life recall is so vivid, and often so unexpected, that it is difficult to deny. Often the experiences we remember explain a lot about the circumstances of our current existence, along with our habits, likes and dislikes.

Double act

The more purified, clear and developed the heart chakra becomes, the better the crown chakra can function. The crown might be the front door to spiritual connection, but the heart chakra is the lock on the door. The key to developing the crown chakra lies inside the heart.

The reason for this is that the core of the crown chakra is an exact replica of the heart chakra. Whatever state the heart chakra is in, it creates the state of being of the core of the crown chakra. If the heart chakra is black and struggling, full of etheric debris and unresolved emotional issues, then the crown chakra is going to struggle somewhat. The vastness of the crown chakra's capacity will not be actualized.

Below on the left is a graphic representation of a heart chakra. On the right is a crown chakra. Notice that the core of the crown chakra is identical to the heart chakra. It is the same in everyone, but few are as light as this. In most there are lumps of unresolved emotional baggage and judgment that prevent clear and full crown activation.

Cleansed heart and crown chakra

Much of the hard work of the spiritual aspirant takes place in clearing, cleansing and building the heart chakra. When the heart develops, then the crown does too.

Yet more chakras: The Soul Star Chakra

Above the crown chakra, approximately 30 centimetres above the head, is another chakra called the 'soul star chakra'. This chakra powerfully connects us to our immense soul self. The antakarana or spiritual cord, runs down through the soul star chakra into the crown chakra, bringing a stream of soul consciousness into our body.

Christ consciousness flows to us through the soul star chakra when we are in a fit state to receive it. For most people this is a process that takes decades of dedication to achieve. Occasionally it can occur in a seemingly spontaneous way, although this is rare. It generally happens through immense good karma and previous spiritual practises in other lifetimes. Usually it happens through being blessed by a powerful spiritual teacher who gives you the grace to develop. Since very advanced Gurus bless the soul body, these blessings last for more than one life. The blessings are like beneficial seeds being planted. Thus, the person who has the 'spontaneous' experience of awakening, may have been a devotee of a particular Guru for one or more lifetimes previously. A seed that may have been planted centuries ago, finally comes of age.

Sweet System

The connection to the soul star chakra grows through the development of the heart and crown chakra. Just as the heart chakra is an exact replica of the inside of the crown chakra, the crown chakra is an exact replica of the inside of the soul star chakra.

The activation of the crown chakra is dependent on the development of the heart chakra. Similarly, the soul star chakra does not really start to operate fully until after the crown chakra has reached a certain level of clarity and development. The more the crown chakra is developed, the greater the role the soul star chakra can play in your life.

As we purify the heart and crown chakras, practice our meditations and raise our vibration, the enormous gifts of the soul star chakra start to be revealed. This design is very clever. Since the crown chakra won't develop to its fullest potential until the heart chakra does, the doorway to God really is through the heart. Thus, the spiritual aspirant is wise to cultivate the promise of the heart chakra, which is a mixture of love, compassion and wisdom. Etheric development of the heart and crown chakras is a key strategy for conscious soul recognition.

Chakras in Action

If the heart and crown are dominant in our consciousness, peace and love will be very important. The heart chakra is about love, kindness, compassion, sharing and empathy. The crown chakra is about inspiration, Divine consciousness and soul guidance. Developing the heart and crown chakras not only develops the sensibilities of the individual, it also develops a mass culture of people who are attuned to peace.

Culturally this is not yet the norm, and the lower chakras are usually more developed than the upper ones. In many cultures there is a lot of emphasis on the development of the solar plexus (putting the self first), because of the importance of competition and winning.

Competition, by its very nature, means that it is either you or me who is going to win. There is nothing wrong with competition, but someone with a developed heart chakra will put limits upon what is acceptable in order to win. Someone *without* a developed heart chakra might not. Society is better off having people with developed heart and solar plexus chakras in positions of authority, as they will be strong and courageous as well as compassionate. They will not be ruthless.

Anger and Soul Connection

When we get really angry, the solar plexus chakra becomes huge in an instant. If one has a tendency to have angry outbursts often, the solar plexus develops as though the person was pumping iron in that region. It gets huge, congested with dirty energy and out of balance with the other centres.

Strong negative emotions like anger actually shut down the crown chakra, thereby cutting off the supply of soul energy coming into our body and energy field. This makes us feel even worse, but it works by stopping unlimited amounts of spiritual power from pouring in through our crown chakra and fuelling the dispute. This is a safety device built into our energy anatomy.

There is nothing wrong if this happens occasionally, but if it is habitual then it negatively impacts conscious soul connection. The voice of the soul cannot be heard when the crown chakra is shut down. The solar plexus' emphasis on winning, being right, and competing will be more important to a person than achieving peace.

How to fix it

After an experience of anger, scan your chakras. How to do this is set out in my book, *Ignite Your Spirit*. You can actually feel for yourself how the solar plexus has become huge and the crown has shrunk. You can use violet flame healing to cleanse your energy field, and this is explained later in this book. If you don't wish to learn yourself, try having an Ignite Your Spirit or Pranic Psychotherapy healing session. It will allow you to gain some perspective over your life and help you to avoid making things worse by an ill considered, angry reaction. You will feel happier, calmer and less egocentric.

Black, Gold, Pink and Green

Depending on the state of development, the heart chakra can clairvoyantly look black and murky, or green, pink or golden. A black heart is one through which very little energy is passing. It is closed down and full of garbage. A green tinge to the heart chakra is called Shanti, or peace. Pink is Prema or love, and gold is a highly activated and Christed heart. In developed people you can also see brilliant blue (like a flame), which is Sathya or truth. Those with golden hearts are people who have an advanced level of soul connection.

Since everyone has been hurt by someone at some stage, all of us carry heaviness in our hearts. Our journey is not to ignore it or project our suffering onto others, but to learn to deal with it, clean it up, and move on.

Heart of Gold

In our culture, a really kind, loving person is described as having 'a heart of gold'. This language is descriptive of the reality. Clairvoyantly those with golden heart chakras glow. The heart chakra actually looks golden, and they emit love. This has been known about for eons, and is why saints and great teachers are depicted with glowing hearts. Such a person is likely to be kind, empathetic, compassionate, giving, caring and loving. Those with large heart chakras find it easy to show appreciation and gratitude to others. They often experience contentment, happiness, peace and harmony.

Even large heart chakras can become congested with heavy energy. This often occurs when there has been a disagreement, dispute, divorce, family feud, war, calamity, estrangement or some other drama. Old emotional pain including grief, sadness, unresolved animosity and judgement, can lodge in the heart like grit and close it down.

Those who have a heart of gold have undoubtedly suffered emotional pain, but have moved on. They have cleared it out through acceptance, forgiveness and an expansion of their ability to love unconditionally. Such people could be called 'emotional Olympians', as they have grown so much through overcoming adversity and suffering. They are not judgemental. They do not just love you if you are good – they love everyone all the time. They are not interested in controlling others, having achieved a Buddha like form of detachment. They are at peace no matter what happens, even though they are aware of the law of cause and effect, and know that actions have consequences. Even if you hurt someone and are jailed, the Golden hearted person will still love you.

Those with golden hearts live fully in the world, and have deep emotions. They feel things acutely, but their feelings do not inhibit love. They can feel content even when they also feel sad. They are calming, spacious people to be around, and you don't have to watch your p's and q's. They are relaxed, and relaxing. Often they find life very amusing and have rich humour. They are extremely empathetic and compassionate. If a friend dies and they are sad, they cry, if they are amused and happy, they laugh. If something angers them, they get over it quickly and do not act or react in a negative way. They rapidly resume their natural state of being, which is happiness and peace.

Cold-hearted

People who are cold hearted don't enter into the realm of emotions at all, usually because it scares them. They lack empathy and don't understand people. Those who have a total aversion towards emotion are not able to develop their heart chakras until they change their habits and their minds. They cannot develop that which they refuse to use.

Given the intensity of emotional energy, they don't want to feel it. Instead they rationalize every situation, and feel safer living just in their head. The irony of this is that the head is the least safe place to live. Sooner or later the universe will present them with circumstances through the agency of change, which they will not be equipped to deal with. They will have to search beyond their own rationality in order to find an answer or solution that makes any sense.

Living just in the head means you don't get involved in what your heart is telling you. The heart is the seat of the soul, and the vehicle through which expanded soul consciousness comes to you. Being blocked from this is not a happy circumstance. It breeds stress, anxiety and depression, which are some of the most prevalent conditions in our culture.

Living in your head means that you fail to enter into the emotional waters. If you don't venture into the water, you can't learn to swim. Refusing to swim up through the astral waters will make it really hard for you to experience the majesty of Soul connection. Love cannot be experienced mentally, any more than sex or chocolate can be. You have to do it, eat it and live it. The heart chakra is the lock on the doorway to the soul, and love is the key.

Resisting Compassion and Empathy

Compassion is being able to feel for the distress or suffering of other people. Empathy is the ability to actually feel what the other person is feeling, even if you have not been told what is going on. Empaths can pick up how other people are feeling just by standing in close physical proximity to them, or through the closeness that comes with relationship.

Many people are natural empaths. They are so attuned to emotional energy that they do not really know whether they are feeling their own feelings or someone else's. This is not as unusual as it might sound. Emotions are not solid, rigid things. They flow like water, and emotional tides are flowing all the time. They flow from and through one person to another. Mass hysteria operates this way. People 'catch' how others are feeling, then they feel it too.

Having compassion and empathy can cause us to make adjustments in our life, because it helps us treat others as we would prefer to be treated.

Unfortunately sometimes having empathy and compassion can be quite painful, and people wish they were not built that way. The stored up pain can get so bad that people close down their heart chakras so as to avoid it. This has the effect of deadening the heart to all emotions, and closing the door to the soul.

WENDY
Wendy was a woman I treated who was very compassionate. She used to watch the news at night, and after a while she became really depressed. The cause of her depression was the extreme suffering that she saw portrayed throughout the world, night after night. At the time there was a lot of coverage of a famine in Africa, with really disturbing images of starving children. She did not want to be on the planet any more, and she did not want to feel this incredible suffering.

Through several healings and attending a Soul Connection workshop, Wendy learnt to reopen her heart chakra. She saw that by closing her heart, she not only avoided the negative emotions, but the enjoyable ones as well. She had become withdrawn and unfeeling because she did not know how to manage her emotions and the thoughts that locked themselves around them. She started to use the violet flame for clearing herself of the energy, and found that she could open her heart to life again.

Closed Hearts

When we cannot forgive people who have hurt us, our heart chakra becomes closed. It gets compacted by negative thoughts filled with emotions ranging from grief, anger, rage, revenge and depression. A closed heart is like a bandage to stop intense pain, but sooner or later the infection under the bandage will have to be treated or it will spread and infect other parts of our body and energy field. If it is left untreated, the old, unresolved pain will reappear every time you get upset. So instead of just getting upset about what is happening in the here and now, all of the old pain will be in your face, and will add huge emotional intensity to a situation that may not actually be that serious. You will suffer from emotional distortion, and will take a small criticism as being deeply offensive and get very angry about it. Past damage that is not resolved leads to over reaction, which keeps snowballing until it is healed. If it is not healed it can lead to a shut down called depression.

Black Heart

Those who are black hearted have been emotionally or physically challenged, and in their rage and anger have become victims to revenge and ruthlessness. They seek power over others as the only way to feel safe. They have a lot of bitterness and hatred. Often they have been very badly damaged either through deprivation, hardship, war, abuse or the negative actions of others, and have not been able to deal with it and recover. The same circumstances that could create a golden heart in one person who deals with the issues, could create blackness in a person who allows the suffering to calcify and go bad inside them.

Black hearted people lack compassion, and because of this they can be cruel and sometimes dangerous. These people have closed hearts which have become more and more blocked. Love is absent. They may experience fondness for others, but their 'loving' is often highly conditional, and they are likely to have knee jerk reactions if those they love do not 'behave' in the way they dictate. Clairvoyantly, their heart chakras look black, because there is no light visible in them. They are closed.

Unrefined Heart and Crown chakra

Those with a black heart chakra experience strong negative emotions for which they generally blame others. They are astrally unstable, and they seek to make things better in a warped and twisted way. The terrorist mentality is an example of black hearted endeavour.

Negative beliefs (creations of the mind, not the heart) are often at the root of black hearts. An example of a negative belief is, "if you hurt me, I have a right to hurt you. I am allowed to be vindictive, because you started it."

On this basis, if you believe that your husband has initiated divorce proceedings and you don't want the marriage to end, you can convince yourself that you have a right to be angry, unreasonable and uncooperative. You will teach him a lesson. I have heard of women cutting up all of their husband's suits after he announces he is leaving. He then thinks you are nuts, and that you cannot behave in a rational manner, so why should he? He then becomes equally demanding and unreasonable. If each side reacts to the other, there can be a scaling up of hostilities, and verbal or physical violence can result. The movie, *War of the Roses* graphically illustrates this point.

A heart filled with love does not react in a violent or negative way to perceived injury from others. They might get upset and feel angry or sad, because people with large, clear hearts are not resistant to feeling emotions. However they do not engage in negative action just because they are feeling an emotion with a low vibration. They feel the feeling, listen to what the emotion is telling them, and then they make a choice as to how they will act. They do their best to practise love and harmlessness.

The beliefs and choices that engender negative behaviour in the world, and the low vibrational emotional that gets trapped, shrink the heart chakra.

As our vibration falls and the heart chakra shrinks, the core of the crown chakra also shrinks. This has the effect of cutting off soul guidance and leading us astray. Because of this, it is really important to look at how beliefs affect us. We will look further at this topic in the astral dimension section, because beliefs are astral phenomena.

People with black hearts are often viewed by those who know them as 'bad' people. This is not accurate. Even those who act in 'evil' ways are Divine children of God, the same as you and me. It's just that some of their choices are rotten! They might be quite jolly in social interaction, but get onto their pet topic and you will see their limitations.

Even really 'good' people can have black spots in their hearts. There are areas in nearly everyone where we find it hard to remain loving no matter what is going on. We judge and condemn, and done repetitively, this is an issue. When you listen to conversations and see how loving they are (or are not) you will get an idea of the light (or lack of it) in the heart of the speaker.

One day in some lifetime or other, all hearts will unblock and humans will be different. This may perhaps occur only after a lot of suffering at the hands of other people, and after experiencing first hand what it is like to be treated the way we have formerly treated others. Sometimes this takes lifetimes. Inevitably, sooner or later we will all get over our blockages to love, our heart chakras will soften and grow, and we will continue our own unique journey into Divine oneness.

Fashion Victim

Whether cold, closed or black hearted, the fashion in emotional management in western culture for centuries was to have a stiff upper lip, to push down your emotions and pretend you don't have them. When the heart is blocked, soul connection is impossible. Men in particular have been held back by this deadening approach. If you refuse to feel emotions and think that it is unmanly to cry, then you may not be using your heart chakra all that much. We are meant to feel emotions, the trick is managing them.

If your heart chakra is not active you may have insufficient energy flowing into your physical heart area. It is not surprising then that heart attack is the most common cause of death in western males. Closed heart chakras are a big factor in heart disease.

One of the reasons that heart disease is hereditary is because the patterns of energy and emotional management are largely given to us by our parents, who play some role in raising us. We naturally learn to be emotionally and energetically like them – it is automatic. If we would prefer not to be energetically or emotionally like our parents, we have to make conscious changes.

When we re-open our hearts, we can once more experience real love, compassion and empathy. When we can feel our emotions and respond to them in an appropriate way, we are better able to manage our life, and Divine connection becomes much easier.

Forgiveness

We all have stories about people who have hurt us, done us wrong and invaded us. These stories range from disputes about where Christmas lunch will be held this year, to horrendous experiences where people have been raped, battered, betrayed and conned. Some people have been through terrible experiences at the hands of others, and look at me like I am mad when I suggest that they try to forgive. They say to me, "If you knew what I had been through you would not ask me to forgive". Actually, I would. Not forgiving someone who has hurt us is like carrying around a ton of coal inside our being. It takes a lot of energy to maintain animosity. This is energy that we could be using for something constructive.

If you really want to, you can find a way to forgive anything. The forgiveness is for us, not just for the other person. Forgiveness sets us free, and allows light as well as love to flow in our hearts. Instead of becoming laden down with emotional baggage, we feel our pain then release it, thereby setting ourselves free. This is what Mr Cobby, in the next story did.

Forgiveness is easier said than done. Even when we mentally know we ought to forgive someone, often we lack the will to actually do it. Forgiveness is more than a mental decision. It means we have to release the trapped energy and emotion.

Often this process happens in waves. It is like peeling the layers of an onion. You take off one layer and think you are finished, but underneath is another layer of stuff that needs to be forgiven. Underneath emotional pain and anger, under the wounding we have received, we will always find love, including for the person who hurt us.

After I got divorced, which was the catalyst for my start on a spiritual path, I found it hard to forgive my husband. Over time, I dealt with more and more layers of the onion. Then one day as I was driving somewhere, and I suddenly realized that I could feel love for my former husband again. I was very excited, because I knew that if I could feel love, it meant I had come a long way with the process of forgiveness.

After you can feel love for a person you need to forgive, there is another step to take. That step is to realize that this person has been your teacher, and has shown you more about your capacity to love than you have ever experienced before.

Karmically, souls travel through time and space together. We have a soul family as well as a biological physical family. The people who we really love, as well as the ones we truly cannot stand, are our soul family. Almost always, someone we need to forgive is a member of our soul family. If we don't forgive them in this life, a similar problem will crop up next time, so that we each learn the lessons that love has to teach us. In the end we realize that, as bad as the experience has been, there is actually nothing to forgive. Then the process is complete, and we are free.

Anita Cobby Killers

In the 1980s there was a horrendous murder committed in New South Wales, Australia. A beautiful woman called Anita Cobby was killed in a gruesome way that involved a lot of torture before she died. The barrister who handled the case was in the same chambers as me.. I remember how this senior and experienced criminal law barrister who had seen it all, was sickened by the evidence in the case.

The most extraordinary thing about the matter was Anita's father. He was naturally devastated by the loss of his daughter in such appalling circumstances. However something remarkable occurred. He chose not to harden his heart and seek vengeance, which lots of people would have done. Instead, he chose to forgive those who had mutilated and killed his child. He even became friendly with the killers whom he visited in prison. He went on to assist many other people who were victims of terrible events such as this. He truly has a heart of gold.

Giving

The heart chakra is greatly strengthened every time we engage in giving. Ensuring that others have enough food, enough money, resources and circumstances for a good life, develops not only your karmic grace, but your heart chakra as well.

Supporting those who heal and teach you about your own Divinity is like paying your power bill. You would not think of failing to pay your electricity account after you use power all month, so do not neglect to support your spiritual teachers for the love and energy that they constantly anchor for you and others. Supporting spiritually advanced teachers, saints and Avatars, assists them to be free to concentrate on their important work of raising the vibration of people and the planet. Supporting them financially develops one of the highest forms of grace in you.

The first time I gave a large amount of money to a spiritually developed and enlightened teacher, I did so merely because he taught us that this was appropriate, and that it would generate the karma of wealth for us. I decided to test the theory. I gave him a big fat cheque, and within 24 hours I had received more than 5 times the amount of money back from a combination of two unexpected gifts. I was stunned. I realized that this was one of the most important things he had ever shared with me, and I was so grateful to be aware of this old truth. It is through giving that we activate the mechanism through which we receive. I had given to him because I wanted to support him, but also to see what happened. Since then I have made regular contributions to my spiritual teachers, even those I have not seen for a while, because without their help I would not have discovered my Divine essence. I am always grateful to them.

Providing the hungry with food ensures we will not go hungry. Providing the homeless with shelter means we will be sheltered. Educating people means that we will be educated, and so on. Giving with true kindness of heart will activate your heart chakra, create positive karma and make you feel good.

Service

Service means a non-financial and non-material contribution to others. It is the use of your own energy to assist others. Generosity, loving kindness, caring for others and helping those less fortunate than ourselves is part of our spiritual opportunity. We the fortunate, have the opportunity to assist those who incarnate and experience difficulty. Through lovingly helping others, we move up the vibrational ladder of life.

If we harden our heart to suffering and decline to help those we could help, we miss important opportunities for our own development. We also miss out on much that is joyful in life, as helping others is a heartfelt, feel good activity.

Helping others from a position of superiority and with an air of judgment, is less beneficial and ought to be avoided. Thinking that we are better than others is a sign of spiritual immaturity, a relatively small heart chakra and a congested solar plexus chakra. It also gives rise to circumstances wherein we will be on the receiving end of someone else's superiority, which is never a comfortable place to be. Through the heart centre we come to appreciate that we are all one. Helping others is really helping ourselves.

Through service our heart chakra grows, and we develop karmic grace. As I discovered when I had a car accident, having a background of serving others provides the wind beneath your wings to lift you up and avoid tragedy.

Every spiritual tradition encourages generosity and service. When you understand that multi-dimensionally speaking, you are giving to yourself, and that you are developing your heart chakra at the same time, you can see why it is so important.

The multi-dimensional world is fluid and constantly in motion. There is no real firm foundation, except our own anchor into the Divine dimension of ourselves. If we won't forgive, if we fail to be generous and think only of our physical self, we cut off our true support, internal guidance and Divine awareness. Only through our intuition, and expansion of the heart chakra, will we know what is really going on and find a way through life that will bring us happiness and peace.

Chapter 10

Developing the Crown Chakra

The crown chakra will not develop any faster than the heart chakra. We have already seen several methods by which we can develop the heart chakra – through giving, forgiving and service. In addition to this, there are four principal ways to develop the crown chakra. These are meditation, prayer, chanting, and being spiritually fed by someone who is already enlightened.

It is also important to clean the crown chakra. The energy of stress builds up all through our energy field, but is particularly likely to get trapped in the crown chakra. Trapped stress energy needs to be released, and methods to manage your stress ought be investigated and implemented. Ignite Your Spirit healing is one of the fastest ways to achieve this. Fortunately, the methods we use to develop the heart and crown chakra will also diminish your stress levels.

Meditation

Meditation is a term that could mean many things. It can be a way to relax, to improve our health, and to reduce stress levels. Meditation can help us to manage emotions more effectively, and to achieve mental focus and clarity[14].

Meditation also allows us to attain direct Divine connection. Every time we meditate, we develop our crown chakra, and the whole process of soul

---

[14] There are many benefits of meditation, refer to forthcoming book *Meditation for Life Enrichment* by Kim Fraser.

connection becomes a little easier. Regular meditation is an important key to attaining and maintaining soul connection.

There are many kinds of meditations. For soul connection, we can chose meditations which are spiritual and energy practices, or we can chose Zen forms of meditation that take us beyond the mind into stillness. Spiritual practices will make Zen meditation easier, especially as Zen meditation is fairly difficult for many Western people to master without a lot of practice.

The most sublime experiences of meditation involve going beyond the mind into a realm of bliss and peacefulness, where you are open to the consciousness of your soul.

Spiritual Practices

Through the use of spiritual practices in meditation, a great deal of spiritual energy comes into your system. This helps you to access a sense of deep peace and insight which assists in managing the many challenges of living in the physical and astral worlds.

A range of meditation CDs which contain profound spiritual practices, are those created by Master Choa Kok Sui, the founder of Pranic Healing. The most amazing one is the *Meditation on Twin Hearts*[15]. This meditation is specifically designed to develop the heart and crown chakras, and has been shown to have a beneficial effect on the lives of those who use it regularly. Scientific studies and research conducted on this meditation have shown measurable changes in the pattern of electrical activity through the brain. Comparing electroencephalograph (EEG) studies before and after meditation, there was a dramatic transition from beta waves to alpha waves and delta-theta waves in 14 meditators and non-meditators[16].

---

[15] This is available through any Pranic Healing teacher or organisation world-wide. Research and scientific studies have been completed on the neurophysiological, psychological and sociological and pycho-spiritual effects of the Meditation on Twin Hearts. These studies have been conducted in the most part by Glenn Mendoza, M.D. in New York City, New York and Dr. Vrunda and Supriya Ghorpadkar and Mr. Sundaram in Bangalore, India.

[16] There was an observable increase in brain synchrony (alpha-delta-theta waves) between the two hemispheres of the brain after the Meditation on Twin Hearts. There was synchronization of brain waves initially between the same hemisphere and followed by synchrony between the frontal, middle and rear portions of the brain. There was a decrease in heart rate and respiratory rate of up to 15-20%, and an increase in oxygen saturation after the Meditation on Twin Hearts. There was significant increase in neurohormones serum Serotonin and plasma Melatonin (up to 300%) following Meditation on Twin Hearts in a pilot study of 17 subjects, and a follow-up study of 35 subjects.

Geoffrey Russell and I have created a range of meditation CDs which contain spiritual practices that can assist you with the process of soul connection. Our *OM* guided meditations are wonderful tools for healing the body and purifying your energy field.

Archangelic Meditation[17] is a very comprehensive guided meditation which takes you into a healing temple. It then guides you through your own self healing, helps you to achieve a quiet mind, and then puts you into a deep state of love. You can bring this peace and love back and bless your entire life with it. Many people, including beginner meditators, find this meditation helps them to connect in a way that they have not been able to do previously. This meditation helps to cleanse away blockages to love, along with other astral blockages that prevent the consciousness of the soul from being heard.

Emptiness Meditations

The second important form of meditation does not involve doing anything in particular, but going beyond your mind. If thoughts come up, you do not focus on them but let them go. If emotions come up you do the same. If your body feels pain you just release it. You go beyond all of that into another dimension. In this state there are no thoughts – just bliss, awareness and peace. You may become aware of a concept or idea, but not in the same way as you would with a thought about a concept. Telling the difference between a thought and pure soul awareness takes practice, but it can be clearly identified once you are used to it.

The focus of emptiness meditations is on nothingness. When you are in the 'beyond mind' state, you feel very spacious and free. Sometimes a conversation will take place with a guide or with your spiritual teacher. This is also different to any other conversation, and does not take place in the same way that we usually hear conversations in our mind, such as when we are remembering something someone said. In an advanced form the dialogue takes place *in your heart chakra*.

Gurus can usually jump start their students into Zen-like emptiness and expanded consciousness, provided the student is receptive. Find one, and see for yourself.

---

[17] By Geoffrey Russell and the author. It is available in English in the UK and Australia, and also available in French, German, Italian, Portuguese, Spanish, Serbian and Croatian. Orders can be placed at www.kimfraser.com and through New World Music in UK and Australia.

Prayer

Prayer has many beneficial effects. Clairvoyantly, those who pray can be observed to be activating their crown chakras. This is a way to develop the crown chakra simply and easily.

Those who pray regularly are creating a strong connection to their souls and the inner Divine world. Over many lifetimes we can develop a huge crown chakra this way.

Prayer sometimes leads to meditation. It can be said that prayer is talking to God and meditation is listening to God. Prayer, being a conversation with God, is personal and individual. Helpful prayers are those expressing gratitude for all of the wonderful things and people in our lives, and prayers asking for help or guidance.

As soon as you pray for something, God sends it to you as energy. It has to come in through your Divine self, down through your soul self, down through your etheric and astral self and then into your physical world. If any of these areas are blocked, you may not be aware of the result of your prayer. You can learn more about this in *Dimensions of Wealth*[18].

As well as making up your own, you can use traditional prayers, which are powerful because of the vast energy they contain from so many people praying on them for so long.

As far as traditional prayers go, I really love 'The Great Invocation' and the 'Prayer of St Francis' which are as follows:

The Great Invocation
From the point of Light within the Mind of God
Let light stream forth into the minds of man.
Let Light descend on Earth.

From the point of Love within the Heart of God
Let love stream forth into the hearts of man.
May Christ return to Earth.

From the centre where the Will of God is known
Let purpose guide the little wills of man –
The purpose which the Masters know and serve.

From the centre which we call the race of men
Let the Plan of Love and Light work out
And may it seal the door where evil dwells.

Let Light and Love and Power restore the Plan on Earth.
Alice Bailey / Djwhal Khul

---

[18] Experiential seminar and forthcoming book by the author.

Prayer of St Francis

Make me an instrument of your peace,
Where there is hatred let me sow love
Where there is injury, pardon
Where there is despair let me bring hope
Where there is doubt, faith
Where there is darkness, light
Where there is sadness, joy
Grant that I seek
not to be consoled but to console,
Not to be understood but to understand,
not to be loved as to love.
For it is in giving that we receive
In pardoning that we are pardoned
It is in dying that we are born to eternal life.

Chanting

Chants are songs of praise which are simple repetitions of the same words and meaning over and over. Chanting is a form of prayer set to music, often involving the repetition of one of the numerous names for God. It is a form of devotion or Bhakti yoga. In *Meditations for Life Enrichment*[19] there is a whole chapter devoted to the whys and wherefores of chanting, and another chapter of chants with translations of the meanings.

Chanting uses sound to progress you on your spiritual journey towards enlightenment. Chanting is fun, and a great way to get people together for healthy interaction. It can be a musical pleasure as well as a spiritual tool.

The cultural or religious background of a chant is irrelevant, unless you happen to have a strong belief in only one religious tradition. I believe that all religions and spiritual paths are different fingers pointing towards the same God. If you believe in the universality of all faiths, as we do at the Harmony Centre, then you can obtain benefit from all forms of chant (and from all of the faiths as well).

Singing about God or great spiritual teachers and saints, strengthens our connection to them. The stronger the connection (which forms through love) the more easily we can be assisted and spiritually fed by them. We become receptive to their Grace.

---

[19] By the author, forthcoming publication in 2007 by Higher Guidance Pty Ltd.

Chanting has the effect of operating like weight lifting for our heart, crown and throat chakras. Various chants affect our energy in specific ways. Some have a cleansing effect, others energize, and so on.

Chants build positive thought loops in your mind too. The high vibration of the chant resounds through your head, and helps you to raise your vibration.

It is not uncommon to have experiences of bliss and expanded consciousness during prolonged chanting. I have experienced my physical teacher speaking to me in my heart during chanting, in a sublime and private form of spiritual instruction.

Food for the Soul

Another method of spiritual feeding is through the help of a spiritual teacher who is already soul infused and monadically active[20]. An enlightened teacher assists his or her students in a similar way to how one lit candle can light many other candles. Such people are rare and precious. If you have the good fortune to find such a teacher, then you are likely to find the process of development much easier. They are generous with their energy and are able to see far more than we can. Their wisdom, born of soul connection, joins them into Divine consciousness, and shows us a way forward. Teachers such as this are sent by God to assist humanity to find their way back into the oneness again. There are as many different kinds of teachers as there are different people.

---

[20] Refer to The Divine And Soul Dimension section for more information about avatars and gurus.

A teacher who is in a physical body is very handy to have, because you get the chance to interact with someone who is already enlightened, and who can demonstrate a more loving way of living. They can also give you amazing activations and blessings when you are ready.

Spirit guides come in a wide variety of vibrational realities. Some spiritual teachers are no longer embodied, yet they are guides to humanity anyway. When we are spiritually young we have smaller guides. As we mature and grow we attract more mature guides. We look at how to work with guides and how to be discerning about this process in our advanced classes.

In every age, the incredible love and generosity of God means that there are enlightened beings on earth to help humanity evolve and grow.

Eventually we will move out of the age of relative darkness (spiritual ignorance) in which we now live, into an incredible golden age of peace and love. This happens as more and more people become developed in their heart and crown chakras, and focus on love, joy, happiness and peace. Our social, economic and political institutions will all be beneficially affected, as they are merely a reflection of the people who form them. All parts of life will become refined and reorganized along higher vibrations of light. Each positive step we take on our own journey of enlightenment makes this reality more likely, and helps bring it into being. Powerful, aren't we?

PART 4
The Astral Dimension

Chapter 11

The Astral Dimension

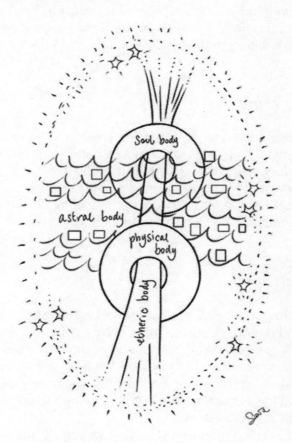

The astral body

Between the soul and the physical dimensions, and interpenetrated by the etheric dimension, is the astral dimension. Just as we have a physical body in the physical dimension, and an etheric body in the etheric dimension, we have an astral body in the astral dimension. The astral body contains our beliefs, imagination and memory, as well as all of our thoughts and emotions.

The astral dimension itself contains the totality of the beliefs, imagination, memory thoughts and emotions of everyone on the planet.

Fully oriented in time and space...

We are usually thinking thoughts and feeling feelings. Our thoughts often have nothing to do with what is currently going on around us. We can be re-experiencing the past, ruminating over what someone said, or worrying about what might go wrong in the future. Often we are oblivious to the present physical moment. Whether we are thinking about the answer to a cross word puzzle, remembering a fight with our boyfriend, imagining what to cook for dinner, or considering how to solve a legal problem, we are in the astral dimension.

We are more consciously present in the astral realm than we are in the physical. In fact, we are astrally engaged nearly all of the time.

A big evolving thing

The astral dimension is huge, and is being created all the time through the continual thoughts, beliefs, expectations and patterns of human interaction. Anything can happen in the astral field. It is the zone that exists between what is *not yet* created in the world, and what *is existing* in the world. It is the dimension that has the most to do with becoming. It is the dimension of reality given to humanity by God to create with.

Receptors or creators?

Thoughts are an important part of what we find in the astral dimension. Many people think of thoughts as arising from events going on around them. In this way thoughts can be viewed as receptors, a bit like senses in the physical dimension. It is certainly handy to be able to think about what is going on around us. Yet this is only the icing on the cake. By using thoughts just to get a handle on what has already happened, people are missing the whole point of being given the power to think!

Thoughts can also function as *instruments of action*. The astral dimension is the cutting edge of creation, and we all unconsciously create things with our thoughts just through the process of thinking, all the time. Usually the process is unconscious, which explains why the astral dimension tends to be in such a big mess.

Positive thinking is a means of getting conscious and concise about what it is you want in your life. By using deliberate positive thoughts, often called affirmations, we can think something into existence if we put in enough effort. We will look some more at that in *Dimensions of Wealth*[21].

---

[21] Forthcoming publication by the author.

What is it made of?

Like everything in creation, the astral dimension and our astral body are made out of energy. Our physical body looks to our physical senses as though it has been created from flesh and blood. However, it is also made out of energy. Instead of being kinetic energy (in motion) it is more dense and static. Such dense, static energy (called matter) gives us the physical world canvas that we recognize.

The astral dimension is made out of a huge vibrational array of emotional energy. Certain forms of angels exist for the purpose of holding a specific, vibrational frequency in place in the astral dimension, and in you. There are angels of peace and angels of conflict. There are angels of hope and angels of despair, as well as angels of happiness and angels of sadness. There are countless Hosts of Angels holding in place the vast creation which is the astral dimension, and all that it contains. From the most exalted vibrations of love and joy, down to the pits of grief, fear and shame, there are bands of emotional energy that form the canvas of the astral dimension. We write our lives on this canvass.

Writing on Walls

Humans have the innate ability to paint pictures and write things in the astral dimension. When the images become strong enough, they can 'fall' into the dense physical dimension[22]. This is how we create things, through the use of our mind.

Once there was a little boy who wanted a puppy. He was not allowed to have one, but this did not stop him imagining that he did. He saved up his pocket money and bought a dog lead. Every day he would take the dog lead for a walk, pretending that there was a dog on the end of it. Then he bought a dog feeding bowl and every night after walking the pretend dog he pretended to feed it. This went on for weeks. In the end, what happened? His parents, who had sworn that they would never get a dog, bought the boy a dog.

A friend of mine, Liz Wilson, once lost 26 kilos in a couple of months without dieting. She just imagined herself thin. She affirmed her ideal weight consistently, and used lots of visualization and affirmation techniques. She ate whatever she wanted to and the weight just fell off her, because her larger physical body no longer matched the slim, gorgeous woman that she was in her thoughts. Amazing but true! Liz now teaches other people how to do this, and you can contact her through the Harmony Centre.[23]

---

[22] This is subject to the laws of other dimensions, and our degree of soul connection.
[23] The Harmony Centre in Cooranbong, NSW, Australia - (02)49 773300

Chapter 12

The devil and the deep blue sea

The astral dimension is very watery. We swim around in the astral sea of thoughts and emotions. It takes some effort to build a pipeline to the soul so that our consciousness can become infused with soul energy. We do this by building our antakarana, as well as developing our heart and crown chakras.

Trying to attain soul connection is like a deep sea diver rising from the sea bed through the sea, on their way to the sun. The sea is like the astral dimension. The diver actually comes from above the sea, but he travels down into the depths to do a job or to have an adventure. At the end of the day he has to get home again. Home is above the water, where the sun burns brightly and warms the air. Home is the soul dimension.

Imagine yourself as the diver in deep water. The sea bed, which is physical, is representative of the physical things of the earth. Divers sometimes find that amazing beauty or adventures captivate them so much that they stay too long and get themselves into trouble. For others, unseen snags, chains or other obstacles trap them and prevent them from moving upwards. Like an unfortunate diver, we can become attached to the physical world and the amazing attractions it holds. We get engrossed here to the exclusion of all else. This prevents us from moving dimensionally upwards.

On top of the sea bed is lots and lots of water. In the depths of the water, there is not much light so it is hard to see, and could be scary. The sea, like the astral dimension, contains no light source of its own. While we are a long way from the light source, certain beings do adjust and live there. These beings are not bad, they are just well adapted to living in the depths.

The astral dimension contains depths such as these which are not particularly pleasant. When we have nightmares, or become infected with very scary thoughts, we are tapping into the murky depths of the astral dimension.

Further up it is less dark, but it can still be murky and unclear. Here it can be difficult to know which way is up. The only way to know would be to watch which way air bubbles rise, and slowly gradually follow them upwards. Watching the direction of the air bubbles is like watching enlightened people. They can teach us how to think and act, along with how to be loving, considerate and peaceful.

Toward the top, the light of the sun can be seen streaming in through the water. There is lots of colour and amazing beauty. The diver might break through the surface into thin air and bright sunlight. Then he is in another realm, just as we are when we break through the astral dimension into the dimension of the soul. It is no longer watery, but fiery. Stay in the sun too long and it can burn you if you are not ready for it. Too much soul energy too soon can burn you, resulting in a condition known as 'kundalini syndrome'.[24]

If you are in the depths of the astral ocean and you want to ascend, then the safest way to do it is to rise slowly. If you ascend too soon when you have dived deep into the sea, you can get the bends. Cleansing, clearing, healing, violet flaming, practicing harmlessness and loving kindness and kindness in thought, will naturally raise you up. With time, planning, persistence and by not continually going back down again, sooner or later we will reach the surface safely.

Due to the relationship between the sea and the sea bed, and because the water sits between the air and the sea bed, we have to get to know the water and be able to swim in it, so as to enjoy life on earth. We even have to get comfortable in, and learn how to manage, the dark and gloomy spaces we might find in the depths. You don't get to fully enjoy the sea bed (life on earth) without learning how to play the astral field like a piano.

If the waters are really turbulent and rough (like the mind often is), we might lose sight of the surface and accidentally head downwards instead of upwards. Through our unbridled thoughts and words, we might accidentally drop like a stone through the astral vibrational reality once more. Then we have to start to ascend again. It may be a little easier than last time, but we have to work our way through the same stuff again.

When we are swimming along, we are in currents of emotion. If we do not fight them, we can get carried along. If we fight against them, we tend to get stuck in them.

The easiest way through all of this is to create your own upward current of high vibrational energy. The soul sends energy to support this journey – all we have to do is to reach up for it. This is a good reason to meditate daily and apply the violet flame to our situation. Instead of getting caught in the current of others, we create our own current of higher guidance.

The Flow

Emotions are fluid. They flow around and through us like tides. They are waves of energy of varying vibrations that we can feel. Some we like, some we don't like. We associate them with certain circumstances, but really they have their

---

[24] This can result in various unpleasant effects ranging from temporary insanity to severe pains, uncontrollable shaking, or burning sensations. For more information on this see *Living with Kundalini* by Gopi Krishna.

own independent existence. Emotions spread, and are not kept inside of our physical self. People can catch emotions from each other in a similar way to catching a cold. Have you ever been around a depressed person and suddenly felt down in the dumps? Or have you felt angry after being in the company of an angry person, or been cheered up in the company of a very jolly person?

Flowing

Since the astral field is very watery, it flows inside, around and through us in a similar way to radio waves.

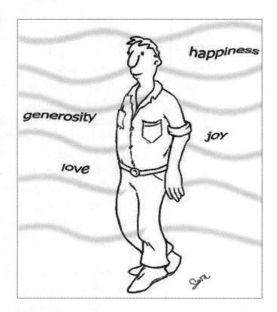

Our astral reality does not stay neatly inside us like our intestines do. We might prefer this to be different, but the reality is that our thoughts, beliefs and emotional makeup leaks out all around us and forms a big blob. Everyone else does this too. Astral energy and vibration passes from one person to another mostly unconsciously. Due to this astral blobbing, the human species is very astrally intermeshed. We are affected by the vibrations of others.

Get 'blobbed' upwards

Given the impact of blobbing, it is important to choose the people with whom you associate carefully. If you hang out with people who are basically degenerate, you will tend to become like them. Their thought forms will mingle with yours, and you may not be able to tell whose are whose. You will grow to be like them.

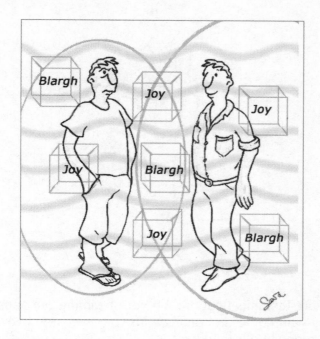

If you want to advance spiritually, it is wise to spend time with people who want the same thing. Find people who are even more advanced than you are, because they will have a beneficial effect on you. Just by being in their company and being 'blobbed' by a high vibrational person, you get lifted up. Try it and see. Belonging to a suitable spiritual community provides an important support network for the budding Initiate, and brings a lot of joy as well. We provide spiritual community at The Harmony Centre, and thousands of people benefit from the interactions that occur there.

Peek-a-boo

Our astral body, including our thoughts and beliefs, can be perceived by others. Usually this awareness of others' astral bodies is unconscious, but with training it can become conscious. *Unconsciously*, every person is aware of what everyone else believes and expects the world to be like. We unconsciously attract to ourselves people and circumstances that match our astral patterning. How the matching takes place is that vibrations in the astral world are attracted to like vibration. By coming together, two or more people co-create reality with each other in a way that matches each person's beliefs and views.

Your dominant thoughts float around you, beaming out your hopes and fears to anyone who comes in contact with you. Everyone knows, on some level, what everyone else is thinking.

Watch out...

Everyone has astral connections with someone. Astral energy flows through these connections and takes thought impressions with it. Because of this, people who are connected with you tend to be aware of what you are thinking and feeling. If you think bad thoughts about a person, don't be surprised if they are a little cool towards you for no obvious reason. They might feel unaccountably irritable with you, because they are reacting to your *thoughts*.

I was once appearing before a wonderful judge who I greatly admired, as he was a very fair and intelligent man. I had known him as a fellow barrister before his appointment to the Court, and was delighted to appear before him on a regular basis. On this particular day I had a difficult case and a difficult opponent. The judge was having a frustrating time of it, as was I. At one stage His Honour tried to steer things in a certain way that I didn't particularly want to go. I angrily thought at him, "I wish you would shut up!" and he said, "There is no need for that language Miss Fraser!" My opponent, who was an emotional block head, heard nothing and looked at us both like we were mad.

The judge had actually heard my thought! It was one thing for *me* to register other peoples' thoughts as I had trained in this area for years, but this judge could do it too! His empathy was very strong, and on that occasion I learned how careful we have to be to control our minds. The bigger you get energetically, the louder your thoughts will resonate all around you. Similarly, the more emotion that is contained in the thought, the clearer it will be received by others.

Communication of our emotion-laden thoughts does not only occur with those in direct physical proximity to us. It occurs through lines of energy to all people anywhere in the world with whom we have a connection. The connection is maintained by thinking about them. Thinking about them causes lines of energy to form. The more you think about them, the fatter the lines become. If your thoughts are of a loving nature, it will be an uplifting connection. If your thoughts are less than loving, you would be better off severing the connection.

You can cut cords of energy. However, it is only through forgiveness that a line of energy can be permanently severed between those who have been in conflict.

Even after the legalities of a divorce are complete, fat lines of energy join people together. If you want to get on with your ex-partner, get them out of your head and stop being so upset with them. Cut the cords! Once the lines of energy are cut, so are co-dependence and conflict. While love cannot be cut, even the most challenging relationship is capable of being improved when the underlying dirty energy and restrictive ties are released.

Telepathy

Thoughts, not being physical, do not just stay inside a person's head. They float around in the astral field. This is why sometimes two people will say exactly the same thing at the same time, or the same thing will be invented at the same time in different parts of the world. Two people have both registered the same idea at the same time, because it was there, floating around, for anyone to think.

We don't tend to think about where thoughts come from, we just think them. This is not wise. The thought voice inside the head is often old thoughts replaying. The voice might be that of a critical parent, or it may be passing thought debris which has blobbed on to you from another person who just walked by. It might even be a thought form loop, like a broken record playing over and over, which commonly occurs in respect of our problems.

Moving On

When people change, the thing that changes the most is their astral bodies. Their beliefs and thoughts change. When this happens, often their friendships change too. They are no longer vibrational matches for the people that they used to associate with. There is nothing to keep them enmeshed any more.

Beliefs are the decisions we have arrived at in order to explain the nature of our reality. Our thoughts often flow from our beliefs. Beliefs can lie submerged beneath our consciousness in the astral dimension. They can often be seen sitting in the aura and can be read by clairvoyants. Often, events can be seen in the aura of a person before they actually happen in the physical life. Most predictions by psychics[25] are merely the logical outcome of the belief boxes that are visible in the person's aura.

If you don't like what a clairvoyant tells you, the good news is you normally have an opportunity to change it, by changing your beliefs and your thoughts. This will always work, provided you have sufficient karmic grace to effect the change.

Floating or getting snagged

When we are emotionally healthy, we do not bury emotions inside us. We just feel and accept them. When we accept our feelings (even negative ones), after a while we float out of that feeling and onto another one. Feelings, being energies in motion, just are, and we get impulsed by them all the time.

When we resist these energies, they get stuck in us. If we resist for long enough, they can even get stuck in the physical body, buried deep down where we might not even be conscious of them. When this happens they can cause disease.

When emotions are trapped inside us, they are usually inside a container. That container is a belief or decision that we have come to. This in turn gets stuck inside various parts of our etheric body. Circumstances are then attracted to us that match our invisible and unconscious astral belief.

You could have an astral belief container that says, "People are generally horrible." So when anyone upsets you, the emotional energy does not go straight through you, but goes into the belief container and fills it up more. This adds more energy to your belief, which increases the likelihood that it will come true tomorrow, or sometime in your future.

If we just had emotions to contend with then, like small children, it would be relatively easy to float from one emotion to the next. Watch toddlers. One minute they are screaming the place down because you will not let them have a chocolate, and the next minute they are all smiles and hugs. Two minutes later they are feeling something else. They have a dispute with you, and after the wave of energy has passed through they revert to being happy again.

---

[25] There are rare people who have full soul connection. They are able to look into the seed of destiny inside you and tell you your probable future. They are not reading thought forms. They are reading the fabric of your soul. There is no mistaking these people because they radiate light, and a positive force field of energy emanates from them.

Toddlers live in the moment, just enjoying the process of being. They have not yet built hornets nests of beliefs which trap their energy, and so emotional energy just flows through them in a natural, healthy way.

Born Free

When we are conceived, mentally and emotionally we are a pretty clean slate.[26] Our past astral nature from previous incarnations is refined and cleansed between lifetimes, and becomes part of our forthcoming karmic patterning. Most of our thoughts and beliefs are released.

During our time in utero prior to birth, we absorb much of the astral reality of our mother. We will experience emotions as she does. Many expectant mothers will tell you that when they are upset, the baby reacts inside of them.

Our beliefs about ourselves and our lives evolve over time. They are registered first as thoughts, flowing from our observation and learning from our early childhood, our family and community. As we get older we absorb further patterns of energy from those around us. Unconsciously we become conditioned to be like those who raised us. Even when we don't like how we were treated, the conditioning happens anyway. Abused kids who hate the abuse, often become abusers. Behaviour patterns, which are founded on beliefs and conditioning (all based on how we think and feel) lie deep within our astral reality, and it takes a conscious effort to change them.

Boxing the flow

Thoughts put little boxes around astral energy. These little boxes fill up with astral waves of emotional energy. These thought boxes are like dams, which stop the emotional energy from calmly drifting away from us, as a wave would seep away from a beach.

When we put emotional energy into a thought and think it a lot, it becomes a thought form. Thought forms are the visible evidence of what would otherwise be called a belief.

---

[26] Likes and dislikes can leak through from one life to another, such as when we instantly feel attracted to or repelled from a particular person. Skills (like Mozart's) and fears (for example, an irrational fear of drowning) can also leak through from one life to another.

Obscuring higher guidance

Our thought forms and beliefs distort the guidance from our souls, just as rain drops distort sunlight. If there are no raindrops, we perceive sunlight as clear light. If there are raindrops, all different colours can form into a rainbow. The rainbow is a reflection of the light hitting an object.

A lot of our thoughts and beliefs act like those raindrops, and change our perception of soul light or consciousness. Often our thoughts are not as pretty as the rain drops, and thus the result is less attractive than a rainbow. A person who has a deep belief that people are out to take advantage of him, will be resistant to guidance that urges him to allow others to love and nurture him. The distortion prevents love and happiness from being his experience. As this area in his psyche is crowded with astral debris rather than joyful soul and Divine energy, his experiences mirror his astral reality (they will not be good) rather than the ever present potential reality of happiness and love.

Creating Space inside for the Soul to come in

Our astral selves are so crowded that, loaded down with all of our judgements, beliefs, expectations and 'knowledge', we have no room to expand into a greater awareness of the possibilities of life and God.

One of the main things we need to do is create spaciousness inside of our energy body, by rubbing out astral stuff we don't need any more. This is like cleaning the blackboard so something else can be written on it. When we do this, we free ourselves up to have more amazing experiences of soul connection and a better life. The more outdated and unhelpful thought boxes we can remove from our aura and chakras, the clearer we will become and the better life will get. As we remove the restrictive thought boxes (or stuck energy containers), the emotions can flow and be released. We feel lighter, and more able to deal with life.

Emotional higher guidance system

The astral energy field, existing mid-way between the soul and the physical dimensions, is the medium through which soul guidance and information reaches us in our ordinary life, particularly in the early stages of our spiritual evolution. The situation changes when we have developed our etheric hardware and our vibration sufficiently, so that instead of relying on that which filters in through the astral dimension, we attain direct Divine connection. This requires a big, strong etheric body, a powerful antakarana and big crown and heart chakras.

Until this extraordinary development occurs, and to some extent afterwards as well, emotional energy is part of the higher guidance system flowing through us. It is the sea through which we perceive the radiant sunlight of Divine consciousness. When we suppress how we feel, we suppress part of our intuitive guidance system.

Thought chatter is another issue that will distort the pure consciousness flowing from the soul and Divine dimensions. This happens because thoughts are things. The more we still the mind and open to our Divine core, the better our reception becomes. We hear our Divine parent, and can recognize ourselves as children of a wonderfully loving God.

Chapter 13

Thoughts

We are thinking (praying) all the time.
We are judging, considering, believing,
deciding, remembering, recollecting, choosing, supposing,
and sometimes focusing. Thoughts can be conscious or unconscious.
They are conscious when we are aware of what is going on in our minds.
They are unconscious when we are on auto pilot, relaxing, driving etc.
Do you know what is in your mind
when you are not deliberately using it to think about something?
Are you able to control the thoughts that are in your mind?
Can you make your mind calm, and can you empty it?
Very few people can fully control their thinking,
and few can rigorously refuse to think
thoughts that are negative,
or lacking in love.
You can learn
to do
this.

Kim Fraser

What is a thought?

A thought is an impulse of energy that registers a meaning for us based on our history of thoughts and experiences, and our overall state of consciousness. If we think a thought often enough, we tend to believe it. Whether the thought is true or not becomes irrelevant. Clever children who are told often enough that they are stupid, often become stupid. We make things true for us by thinking and believing them.

Thoughts affect our reality because thoughts mould and change energy into different shapes. Thoughts are like templates – they cause patterns of energy to form, and because of this they are really powerful.

"What makes up things…
are ideas, concepts, information."
– Fred Alan Wolf, Ph.D[27]

---

[27] *The Little Book of Bleeps*, no page numbers: look near the front.

Review your Thought Diet

When looking at nutrition we often use a food pyramid to describe how much of certain types of foods we should eat for good physical health. At the bottom is roughage, grains and fibre. Above this are fruit and vegetables, above that is protein, and above that are fats and oily food. If we must eat sugary junk food, it is a tiny bit at the top of the pyramid.

For good spiritual and mental health, we are better off having the majority of our diet made up of good and wholesome thoughts. Next, we chose ordinary, functioning thoughts, like the thought involved in carrying out tasks. If we must have negative thoughts, they ought to comprise only a tiny sliver at the top of the pyramid.

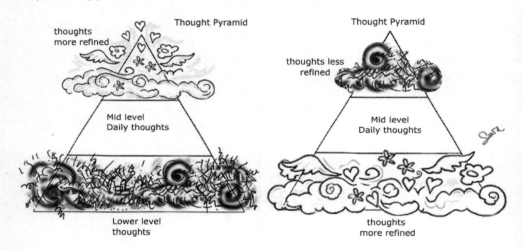

Many people have reverse thought pyramids, and most of the time they are thinking about garbage. Negative thinking is a spiritual condition that can be treated. When we seek to eliminate negative thinking, we are more able to create futures which will be wholesome and enjoyable. We will raise our vibration and float into soul consciousness almost as a matter of course.

Static

Thinking a thought, if done repeatedly, causes a pattern just like the thought to be established in the astral plane within your astral body. Some of these patterns, created by random, stray thoughts, are like static. Static arising from the billions of thoughts and beliefs that we have, creates billions of tiny grey bits of energetic 'dandruff' that sit in our aura and fog it up. The more this happens, the less clear we become. Over time this can dirty our aura, slow down our energy flows, and make it harder to expand our consciousness.

On the whole, peoples' minds contain a whole lot of thought chatter and inconsistent garbage that should be deleted, like emptying the recycle bin in your computer.

Even really smart, well educated people suffer from this problem. When your mind is full of chatter and the 'inner critic' is going at full speed, there cannot be peace. When you try to relax or go to sleep, sometimes there is an endless assortment of thought static flowing through your mind. It seems to play by itself, and is quite hard to stop without knowledge of the appropriate tools. Like fire, the mind makes a great servant but a terrible master.

What signs do I wear?

Our thoughts exist as forms or pictures in our astral body and, as mentioned earlier, our dominant thoughts are visible to clairvoyants. These thought forms become the template through which your life experience is poured.

What pictures have you created in your aura?   Do you want to keep them or adopt another more beneficial set?

Just stop now and answer the following questions. Take your time, and try to be honest with yourself about the things you habitually think.

Thought Assessment

I spend a lot of time thinking about…
When I want to relax I like to think about….
I find it hard to turn off because my mind becomes focussed on…
When I am not really concentrating, I catch myself thinking about…
My stress level on a scale of one to ten, where one is peace and ten is rampant anxiety, is…
The main problems that I think about are…
My 'inner critic' often says to me…
The most challenging relationships in my life are with…
My dominant thoughts in respect of that / those people are…

Later we will see how to remove negative thoughts, and you can refer back to this table and choose some to practice on.

Apart from causing stress, negative thoughts and emotional baggage can distort what your higher self is trying to tell you. Soul guidance is above our astral body like scenery is around and above a lake. If you could only look at the lake, you would know what the scenery was like because you can see it reflected in the lake. If the lake is dirty and rough, you can't see anything.

Thought static and thought forms obscure higher guidance in the same way that wind ruffling the surface of a lake would make it impossible to see a reflection of the surrounding scenery. Rid yourself of the thoughts (or the wind) and the reflection, which gives you a lot of useful information, becomes visible.

If we have enough willpower and time, we can train our brains not to dwell on negative thoughts. We can eventually eliminate them. Insist that your mind not dwell on problems and ask your Divine parent for help with a solution. Ask, *"What is the highest vibrational possible outcome in this situation?"* Then stop thinking about it. Allow a solution to be sent to you from a higher level of consciousness. Go and relax, take a shower, listen to music, meditate, and allow the spark of genius consciousness that lies dormant within everyone to ignite.

Violet flame purification techniques use energy from your soul to cleanse your mind and astral body. The use of violet flame purification techniques can vastly speed up a change in consciousness and give you the internal space for conscious, clear soul connection. A by-product of this process is a still mind and deep inner peace.

PART 5
Healing the Astral Body
using the Antakarana
and Violet Flame

Chapter 14

Soul, Thought and the Violet Flame

Soul consciousness

The consciousness of the higher soul is resplendent with wisdom and love. Normal astral consciousness is only what we believe it to be. To live on Earth and deal with the physical reality, it is desirable to learn to pull the awareness we gain from our soul through to the physical dimension, without it getting distorted in the astral dimension. We will make better decisions, our minds will be clearer, we will be calmer and ultimately we will be happier.

In this chapter we are going to look at various etheric and astral means through which you can strengthen your Divine connection, and clean up your astral body at the same time.

Soul consciousness Super highway

As we saw earlier, when we incarnate our Higher Soul 'pours' a portion of itself down from the Soul dimension, and through the astral and etheric dimensions so that we can take on a body and have a physical incarnation.

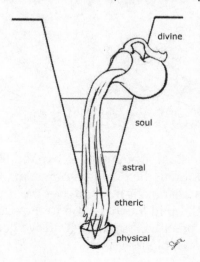

What it actually flows down through is the part of our etheric body known as the 'antakarana'. This is also known as the pillar of light. It is a part of the etheric body, and it is like a soul consciousness super highway.

The Pillar of Light

The antakarana flows down through the core of our body. It comes in through the soul star chakra about one foot above our head. It enters the body through the crown chakra, and then runs out through the body into the core of the earth. When we activate this column of light, we look like a big pillar of light that joins heaven (the inner world) to Earth (the outer world). The expression 'pillar of the church' comes from the spiritual pillar that exists within all of us, but which is greatly developed in the spiritually mature.

In most people, the pillar of light is pretty hard to distinguish, and can resemble threads of cotton rather than a pillar. Such a small receiving apparatus will make it really difficult, if not impossible, to have conscious soul connection. It would be like trying to lift 300 kilos when you don't have a crane to help you.

Part of our job as spiritual aspirants is to expand the pillar. The pillar can be rapidly developed through the practices of healing, prayer and meditation. Strand by strand, the antakarana is built up over thousands of incarnations. As we, the incarnated soul, build a connection to the soul, the soul will answer us. It can take a bit of practice, but in the end we get clear connection and become one with our own higher guidance.

Here is a wonderful exercise to quickly develop the antakarana. It is one of the most profound meditations that I know, and it builds the antakarana by strengthening both ends of it.

Pillar of light meditation

The pillar of light meditation is powerful and strengthening. It connects us to Earth (the outer world) and to heaven (the inner world). It brings balance to our auras, strengthens the energy fields, and develops our pillar of light meridian. It centers us very quickly, and develops the crown chakra as well as our connection to the Earth.

EXERCISE: PILLAR OF LIGHT MEDITATION

1. *Place your tongue on your palette so that the underside of the tip of the tongue is against the roof of the mouth, joining up the micro-cosmic orbit.*

2. *Breathe in, and as you release the breath, imagine it leaving your body through the base chakra and going deep into the earth.*

3. *With the next in-breath, breathe in through the base chakra and into the pillar of light meridian. Imagine the healthy, pure earth energy coursing up through the core of your body, out through the top of your head (crown chakra) and up through the many chakras that exist between the crown chakra and the Supreme God. Imagine it travel through all of your subtle bodies and all dimensions. Feel the energy move.*

4. *With the next in-breath, breathe in energy from God/Goddess, bring it down through the many chakras above your head, in through the soul star and crown chakras, down through the pillar of light meridian and out through the base chakra into the earth.*

5. *Repeat the cycle (steps 2 and 3) between three to seven times.*

6. *End the practice by bringing energy up from the earth to the heart chakra.*

7. *Say either out loud or to yourself: "I am grounded and connected to the Earth. I am one with God and one with all. I am a Divine being of love. I am one with my higher soul. Through the grace of God, so be it."*

Building the Antakarana

Regular practice of the meditation set out above will develop your pillar of light. Sai Baba says this is one of the most important forms of meditation. It does not have to take a long time. You can do it in minutes. If you connect in this way to your higher soul and to the earth every day, you are developing the super highway through which the magnificence of your soul can infuse your etheric, astral and physical self.

What happens next

When the antakarana is very developed and is being used to bring in Divine energy, it resembles a large vertical spiral. The antakarana swells and spreads out into the aura with a brilliant core like a vortex. Energy flows all around. This flaring of the antakarana allows for a great deal of refined energy to come into the energy field. The energy that comes in through the etheric body from the Soul and Divine dimension is somewhat electric and radiates outwards, beneficially affecting anyone who comes within its orbit. It feels like a force field of radiant light and energy and brings with it access to a great deal of knowing through direct perception rather than through any usual form of learning. The soul consciousness super-highway is in full swing.

Antakarana and Violet Flame Soul Energy

The bigger your antakarana, the more soul energy can pour into your body. This makes you more soul-infused, more spiritually aware, and far more potent as a person. When you can make use of your antakarana in a conscious way, you can bring in violet flame energy to create miracles of healing for yourself and others.

Violet Flame Energy

The Violet flame is a form of soul energy that is available to us through our intention to invoke it. It comes in through our antakarana.

Violet flame is not the same as the pranic energy from air, earth, water or the sun. Earthly prana is essential for our physical well-being but is of a totally different quality.

If we wish to make mental and emotional changes reasonably quickly, the fastest way to achieve this is to use soul energy. Violet flame (soul energy) is hugely intelligent. It is powerful, and it is so bright that it cannot easily be looked at. It resembles the brilliant light given off when someone is using a welding machine. It is electric white, with brilliant, incandescent tinges of violet. St Germain is associated with the use of the violet flame.

Using violet flame for healing

The violet flame can be used to effect miraculous treatment for a whole range of ailments. It can wipe out negative thought forms and repair damaged energy anatomy. It can dissolve emotional blockages, and heal relationships. It is a truly Divine tool.

The way in which we can use energy for healing is set out in my previous book, Ignite Your Spirit. Should you wish to understand the process more fully, please refer to that publication.

Before we start to work with the violet flame for specific healing applications, we will look at a summarized version of how to Ignite Your Spirit.

10 Steps to Ignite Your Spirit

First, grab a plastic container and put some water and a couple of tablespoons of salt in it.[28] Have it next to your patient so that you can flick energy garbage into it. Now you are ready to start.

TEN STEPS TO IGNITE YOUR SPIRIT
1. Invoke
2. Connect
3. Perceive
4. Add energy
5. Clean
6. Check
7. Bless
8. Seal
9. Cut
10. Give thanks

STEP 1: INVOKE
An invocation is a request to the Divine to help you to do something. Prior to doing anything involving healing, I always invoke. A simple invocation is:

"I call on God, Divine Father and Mother.
Thank you for being here and sharing with us
healing, light, love, wisdom, guidance and protection.
Through your Grace, so be it."

Invocation provides protection by surrounding you with high vibrational energy, which flows from the non-physical beings that you invoke.

Here is a longer form of invocation, to which you can add as you feel is appropriate. Focus on the crown chakra and the meaning of the words as you say them.

Invocation
I call on the Supreme God, Divine Father and Mother
I call on my Soul and Divine Self
I call on all of my guides, teachers and friends in the Spiritual Hierarchy
I call on [name particular teachers, for example Jesus, Sai Baba]
I call on the Healing Angels and Spiritual Helpers
Thank you for being here and sharing with us healing, light, love, guidance
and protection
May I be a clear channel for light, love, power and healing energy.
Through the grace of God, so be it.

---

[28] Refer to page 199 of *Ignite Your Spirit* for further explanation.

If you are Christian you can call on Jesus, Mother Mary or any of the Christian angelic beings and saints. If you are Buddhist you can call on Buddha or Quan Yin. If you are Hindu, call on Krishna, Brahma, Vishnu, Paravarti, Ganesh or any one of the hundreds of other deities, and so on.

Every time we invoke, we increase our own vibration and form stronger connections with these loving beings. When I invoke, I feel a tingling sensation on my crown chakra, like being out in the rain or under a waterfall, but it is not cold.

We also call on our own soul and Divine self, not because they are absent and need to be called in. It is to increase our awareness of that immense part of who we are, and to strengthen our conscious connection there. Invoking also provides a safety belt, in that the Holy Beings we ask to send energy for healing will help ensure that we do it properly and safely.

STEP 2: CONNECT

This means to be aware of your connection to your Higher Self. This is achieved through awareness and activation of the antakarana. To carry out effective healing for ourselves or others, we need to be strongly anchored into our soul self, and increasingly aware of this level of reality.

The pillar of light meditation that was outlined earlier, is one way to have our feet on the ground and our head in the world of our spirit at the same time. It is an easy process and a good one to do daily, as it only takes a couple of minutes. You are advised to perform that meditation as a means to connect prior to commencing any healing work. It need take only a few seconds.

By choosing to consciously connect like this before you start a healing, you are maximizing the amount of energy you are capable of bringing in from your soul through your antakarana. It makes you stronger. It will develop you. It also makes a big difference to the outcome of a healing.

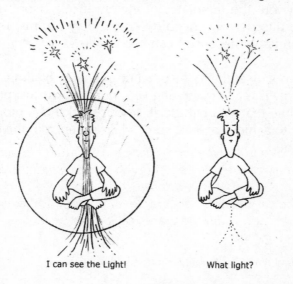

I can see the Light!   What light?

If you do not connect before carrying out healing, you might be using plain air prana rather than soul prana for the job. It is less effective that way.

This process will soon become second nature. After invoking and connecting, you are ready to start the healing.

STEP 3: PERCEIVE

This step in the process of healing involves an assessment of the energy anatomy of your patient. We want to know the state of the aura and of the chakras, their relative size, and state of congestion (being filled with garbage) or depletion (when they have run out of energy).

Some people take in stimuli visually, some are auditory learners, and some are tactile. The same is true of inner plane perception. Most people are able to perceive the inner world if they really want to, provided they are willing to practice. The practice of perceiving energy during Ignite Your Spirit healing will help you to develop clairvoyance (seeing energy), clairaudience (hearing energy) and clairsentience (feeling energy with your hands and body). It is no harder than learning to play the piano or drive a car.

For most people, clairsentience, or feeling energy with the hands, is the easiest method. This is sometimes called *scanning*. The sensations are subtle, and at first we may think we are just imagining things. With practice however, we develop acute sensitivity to energy and can tell a lot about our patient through stopping to perceive how things are prior to a healing.

When I first started I was hopeless at this. I couldn't see, feel or hear anything. I could wave my hands around in complete oblivion, but the interesting thing was that people said they felt better afterwards. Even though I had very little idea of what I was doing, it was working. It took me a good eighteen months to develop much sensitivity to energy, however I found that the more I practiced, the better I became. Eventually I was able to perceive not only energy, but the templates of energy in a person's auric field and chakras. I learned to perceive peoples' core thought forms. This ability to go to the core of an issue (because I can see it) allows for very deep healing to occur.

Perceiving is not essential to the practice of energy healing. If trying to feel, see or hear energy is really frustrating you, don't worry. Just practice and you will find over time that you can do it. In our workshops more than 90% of people are able to achieve at least some clairsentience in the first weekend (I was a slow learner).

HOW TO SCAN

Rub your hands together to get energy to flow through the minor chakras which exist in the palms of your hand. Shake your arms and roll your shoulders. Let your body relax. Open and close your fists then rub your hands some more. Raise your hands and scan the aura of the patient.

Close your eyes and let your hands find the outer edge of the aura. When you feel it, you may experience a slight change in temperature, or a feeling of

fizzing or buzzing in your hands. You might feel a prickly sensation, or your hands might start to feel warm or cold. Make a mental note of how it feels, whether it is firm like pressing on a balloon, or if it feels prickly, or soft and fluffy.

Open your arms and scan the diameter of each chakra as you go down the front of the body. This is a little easier than feeling for the aura, as the energy of the chakras is generally denser and easier to feel. You may feel heat, prickling, thickness, or just a sense of energy when you connect with the circumference of the chakra.

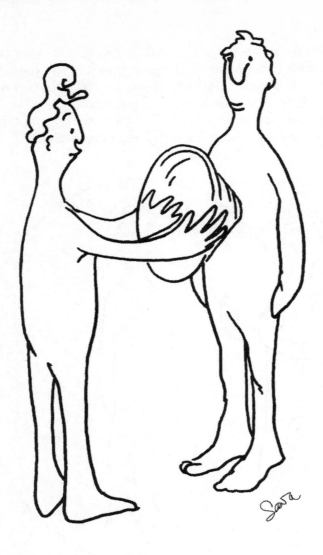

Begin with the crown chakra, and do not worry about the soul star chakra at this stage. After scanning the diameter of the crown chakra, then feel for the ajna between the eyebrows, feel the throat chakra, and so on down the front of the body. Intend which one you are feeling for, and refer to the map of the chakras below as a reminder of where they are.

Then go behind the person and scan the back of the chakras – the meng mein and base chakras. Make a note of your findings. The meng mein should be no more than half the size of the other chakras in diameter. If it is bigger than that the person may have high blood pressure. You should not bless either the meng mein or the base chakra if that is the case, because you don't want to make them even bigger.

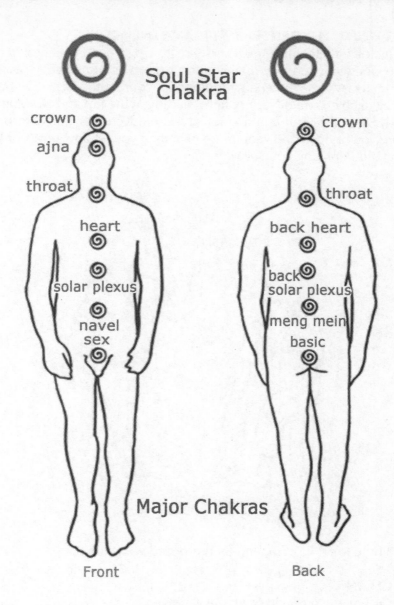

Soul Star Chakra

crown
ajna
throat
heart
solar plexus
navel
sex

crown
throat
back heart
back solar plexus
meng mein
basic

Major Chakras

Front

Back

STEP 4: ADD ENERGY

When we have to remove dirt from something in the physical world, we often put a solvent on it to loosen it up and make cleaning easier. When we have dirt in the energy body we can't use soap, but we can use a certain type of energy to cut through it so we can easily sweep it away. To place energy in the body, we just intend to do so, and the energy will follow the thought.

To add an energy solvent for healing we can use either light or sound. To cleanse ourselves or our patients astrally, we use the violet flame.

ADDING LIGHT: ELECTRIC VIOLET FLAME ENERGY

To add electric violet flame energy, first breathe in through your crown chakra as you do when you connect. Imagine that you are bringing light in from your soul star chakra. Allow the energy to flow out your hands. Visualize painting or spraying each chakra of your patient, starting at the top and working down their body, just like you would spray stain remover on a dirty trouser leg. Make sure you bring in and keep more light than you let flow out your hands, so as to avoid depleting yourself.

Wait a minute to let it set in, and then proceed with step 5.

STEP 5: CLEAN
Now we are ready to get rid of all the garbage.

ORDER OUT THE MESS
Connect again, and ask your patient to repeat after you:

> "I command …. that all negative energy,… negative thoughts,…
> negative emotions,… and negative vibrations… leave my
> body… through all time,… space… and lifetimes. …Through
> the grace of God…and my own will,… So be it."

Ask your patient to Breathe in, and release.
Repeat this three times.

CLEANSING WITH YOUR HANDS: SWEEPING

Having now properly loosened the energetic garbage, and instructed it to leave the body, you can now remove dirty energy with your hands. Normally you can do this with a sweeping motion, as though you are dusting with a damp cloth and then shaking it (your hands) out into the salt water. Sweep their whole body and aura thoroughly, from top to toe. You can keep your fingers closed sometimes, and then slightly apart during other times. You can also sweep any particular areas or parts of the body that are causing pain or discomfort.

Cleaning out clouds of astral debris from the chakra

A clean and activated chakra

As you are sweeping, sometimes you will come across energy blockages that feel or look like ropes, strings, sticks, pieces of metal or other strange things. Simply pull this dirty energy out of the energy centers and the aura and throw them into the salt water. Be thorough, as this is one of the most important parts of the healing process and should take the most time.

Throw or flick the garbage you are removing into your salt water container. Make sure you do not allow the stuff to stay on your skin as it might seep in. Shake your hands over the container of salty water with a flicking motion. You can use rubbing alcohol, lavender essential oil, or soap and water to thoroughly clean your hands. Ensure you do this again after the healing is complete.

STEP 6: CHECK

Rescan your patient to see whether the chakras now feel fairly clean, and whether or not they have completely come into balance. Sometimes they will have, other times they may not. If they still feel prickly, then simply repeat steps 4, 5 and 6 several times until the prickly sensation is gone. By this time any pain or discomfort that your patient may have felt, will most likely have disappeared.

STEP 7: BLESS

To bless people, bring in some of the endless supply of Divine energy in the same way that you brought it in during step 4 above. Feel the energy coming down through your crown chakra from your soul. You may experience a tingling sensation, or an expansion of your crown chakra as you do this.

When you are conscious of a lot of energy in the crown chakra, start to release some of it out your hands and toward the patient. At the same time, ask that they be blessed. You can say:

> *"I ask that you be blessed with healing energy. May this be*
> *distributed thoroughly and completely throughout your body*
> *and energy body. Through the grace of God, so be it."*

Visualize energy entering the whole of their aura, and bringing balance to their chakras. Get them to breathe in and hold as long as they comfortably can, then breathe normally.

Ask that they breathe the blessing into the physical body, so that the energy fills every cell. Then ask them to breathe deeply, bringing the energy into the astral body with their intention. Then ask that they breathe deeply and intend that the blessing and energy fill the etheric body. Then, ask that they breathe normally.

If a specific part of the energy body is weak or damaged, focus energy there so as to strengthen that particular area. Remember that the meng mein should only be half the size of the others. Unless you are an experienced healer you should not bless it directly as the energy will be too strong.

To give an example, let us imagine that the solar plexus chakra feels too small compared to the others, even after you have done lots of cleaning. It may feel too small because there is insufficient energy in it, and we therefore need to deliberately add more. You do this by specifically directing a blessing toward it.

For any chakras that appear undersized, you can direct energy into them. Or, for a stronger result, you can energize them with a supporting affirmation. When you know the purpose of each chakra, you can direct specific blessings into them for well-being and good health. For more information on this, refer to *Ignite Your Spirit*[29].

When blessing people with energy, it is not supposed to be your own energy that you are using. If you use your own much needed vital energy, you will soon get depleted and become weak or sick yourself. Instead, use energy that you draw in and only project between 60% and 70% of the energy to your patient. This way you keep some energy for yourself, and still do a great job for your patient.

WARNING

You should never directly energize and bless five different regions of the body. These are the:

1. front of the heart chakra – concentrated energy put straight into the front of the heart can cause serious heart problems.

2. eyes,

3. spleen,

4. meng mein,

5. belly of a pregnant woman. Directed Divine energy is too strong for the foetus.

The eyes, spleen and meng mein are delicate and should not be blasted with energy. Just clean them.

---

[29] Refer to page 199 of *Ignite Your Spirit* for further explanation.

STEP 8: SEAL

Working in someone's etheric body opens it up. This is safe to do because we have invoked for Divine protection and help. At the end of the healing we need to close it again. This keeps all the new clean energy in, and potential dirty energy contamination out.

To seal the energy field, imagine placing a sky blue eggshell of energy around the aura. This will prevent the energy that has just been added from dissipating, and will seal the aura energetically

Around the blue shell, place a golden, bright criss-cross mesh. This is like a semi-permeable membrane, allowing all negative garbage to continue to flow out, but not allowing any in. All negativity must stay outside of it. Tell it this is its job. Creating a seal around the aura in this way is very powerful.

To allow the person to continue to drain off any negativity that may still be flowing out, it is important to stipulate clearly that the shell is to be semi-permeable. Otherwise their own garbage can rattle around inside this shell and will not be able to escape. This will feel horrible.

Around all that, place an electric violet flame, like a gas flame licking the outside of the egg. This will also assist in the burning off of any negative energy that may come towards the person over the next few weeks.

As you create this triple-layered energy shell, think or say:

> "Seal the aura. I command that this shield will stay in place for one week. It shall protect you from all negative influences. All negative thoughts vibrations emotions and energies can flow out but not in. Through the Grace of God, so be it."

If a chakra is particularly weak or needed a big blessing, you can place the same type of shell on it, using the same method. Instead of placing the shell around the aura, place it like a cap over the end of the chakra. Intend that the energy be used to create the shell on that chakra and it will happen.

STEP 9: CUT

During healings, energy lines form between you and your client. If you do not cut them, any time the client thinks of you he or she can pull energy from you through these energy lines. When you have a lot of clients and do healing for a long time, this is not an option for your continued good health. To avoid depletion, cut from those to whom you have given healing.

Cutting can be done by every professional person after every consultation to minimize the amount of energy that a client draws out of you. It doesn't matter if you are an accountant, psychologist, doctor, nurse, lawyer or healer, you can practice cutting from your clients after they leave. You will be amazed at what a difference this makes to your energy levels.

Cutting is really simple. Use your hand like a sword to cut down the front of your body and say, "Cut." You may want to do this a few times. If you anchor violet flame while you do it, it will be 10 times more effective.

STEP 10: GIVE THANKS

Since you have asked for help to perform the healing, it is appropriate to give thanks for it at the end. This shows goodwill and respect, and reminds us that we are only the pointy end of a great big, Divinely inspired healing team.

Practice makes stronger

Often when students start to work with the violet flame, the amount of energy that is available is not huge. This is because the ability to use the violet flame depends upon the degree of the development of the healer. The bigger the antakarana, the more the flow can cascade into the energy body of the healer, and then into the client.

It is necessary to practise working with soul energy. The more often you do this, the stronger and better at it you will become.

Use of the *Archangelic Meditation* CD and doing the pillar of light meditation will facilitate this practice, and help you to grow both your crown chakra and your antakarana.

Don't mix and match

If you are used to working with colour prana, do not mix it with powerful electric violet soul energy. It can have all kinds of effects that can be dangerous. Just use electric violet brought in through your crown chakra. For detailed information about how to heal physical ailments and mental conditions using the violet flame, see Pranic Psychotherapy and Advanced Pranic Healing by Master Choa Kok Sui. Later in this book we will be looking primarily at how to manage stress, develop better relationships and live in peace. As this occurs many health problems, including serious and chronic ailments, may spontaneously disappear.

Chapter 15

Specific Applications for the Violet Flame

How to Scan for Positive or Negative Statements

A statement or belief can be measured to see whether it is negative or positive for the person who says or believes it. If it is positive, it will make their energy body bigger. If it is negative, it will make their energy body shrink.

1. Rub your hands together to get energy to flow through the minor chakras which exist in the palms of your hands.

2. Raise your hands and scan the aura of the patient. Make a mental note of the size and how it feels (whether it is firm like pressing on a balloon, or prickly or soft).

3. Make an affirmative statement. For example, try saying *"God does not exist."*

4. Note the change in the energy field. See whether the energy in the aura grows or shrinks.

5. If the energy has shrunk, make the opposite statement. *"God exists and I am connected to God"* and see what happens.

6. Always finish this exercise having found a statement that is positive.

7. Stabilize the energy.

8. Cut.

Testing for the effect of the violet flame on our crown chakra

The following simple exercise demonstrates the beneficial strengthening effect that the violet flame has on our crown chakra.

Exercise: Anchoring the violet flame.

1. Work with a partner, and decide who will be the participant in the experiment and who will be the scanner (you will swap later and repeat the process).

2. Scanner, scan the energy in the crown chakra of the participant, noting the size and consistency of the energy.

3. Ask the participant to bring in energy from the surrounding air.

4. Scan the energy in the crown chakra of the participant as they bring in energy from the surrounding air. Notice any change. Then ask them to stop.

5. This time ask the participant to bring in Violet flame energy from the Soul,

6. Scan the energy in the crown chakra as they bring in Violet flame energy from the Soul.

7. Scan the energy in the crown chakra as the participant says "I am one with the Violet Flame."

8. Notice any change in the size, quality and density of the energy in the crown chakra.

9. Swap.

10. Discuss your experiences.

TESTING 100% INFLOW, 60% OUTFLOW

When working with energy it is really important not to deplete ourselves. This exercise is meant to give people feedback as to whether they are unwittingly doing so. If the exercise is done properly, the crown chakra of the participant will not diminish as this task is completed. If it diminishes, they are releasing too much energy and should be told to adjust the flow so as to keep more for themselves. This is all done through will or intention.

1. Scan the crown chakra of the participant.

2. Ask them to anchor the violet flame, as in the above exercise.

3. Ask the participant to raise their hands with the palms facing downwards towards the ground, and to release 60% of the energy they are bringing in to bless the Earth.

4. Scan the energy in their crown chakra as they release 60 % of this energy through the hands. The crown chakra should continue to grow while this occurs, because 40% of the energy ought to be retained. If the crown chakra shrinks, let them know that they are making a technical error in giving too much, and direct them to keep more energy for themselves. Done occasionally there is no problem but done as a matter of course during hundreds of thousands of healings, a person who gets this wrong can become depleted.

5. Swap.

6. Discuss your experiences.

Chapter 16

Mental Renovation for a Better Life

Thought Vibration and Soul Connection

Souls vibrate at a very high vibration. Stress, anxiety, worry, guilt, shame, blame and misery are experienced when we are vibrating at a low level.

Negative thoughts lower our vibration and can make our lives a nightmare. In severe cases negative thoughts can become obsessive or compulsive. For instance, following severe trauma such as being raped, attacked or being in a car accident, it is not uncommon for people to have flashbacks.

To raise our vibration, we need to rid ourselves of negative thought habits, self sabotaging thoughts and culturally conditioned limitations. We replace them with positive energy. When we start to think at a higher vibration (and our thoughts reflect love and respect for the self and others) our overall vibration improves. We naturally move closer to the shining bright, high voltage, high vibrational consciousness of our soul. The side effect of this is that our lives become much happier.

RUTH

Ruth was in a terrible car accident. She was in the front seat of a car travelling on a country road which was involved in a high speed accident involving a truck. Everyone in the car was injured, and a passenger in the rear was killed in the impact. The car was a total wreck.

Ruth was a well-adjusted, intelligent person who had never suffered from any kind of psychological or psychiatric problem. Following the accident she had whiplash and a broken rib. These things healed, but what did not heal was her mind. She had trouble sleeping because when her mind was not kept busy, she repeatedly saw vivid images of the accident play over in her head.

Given that Ruth had been in a shocking and emotionally charged situation, her thoughts at the time became filled with those strong emotions and frozen into little boxes in her energy field. I saw Ruth several times over the course of a month, and on each occasion we did an Ignite Your Spirit Healing, including the following treatment which is very effective for dissolving troublesome thoughts. Ruth was able to release a great deal of the emotional pressure from the thought and, in the end, the accident became a distant and neutral memory rather than a powerfully disturbing thought. She no longer has nightmares and her sleep patterns returned to normal.

Exercise: Getting rid of negative thoughts

The first step in this process is to give the person a complete healing. To refresh your memory, the **ten steps to Ignite Your Spirit** are:

1. Invoke
2. Connect
3. Perceive
4. Add energy
5. Clean
6. Check
7. Bless
8. Seal
9. Cut
10. Give thanks

After performing an Ignite Your Spirit healing as set out above, proceed as follows.

Get your patient to choose a thought about herself that she would like to get rid of. The exercise in Chapter 14 asked you to look closely at your thoughts, so perhaps you could ask them to do that and find something that they would like to work through.

1. Discuss how this thought affects the patient.
2. Ask your client to tell you, on a scale of 0 to 10 (where 10 is an overwhelming thought and 0 is unable to think the thought), how big the troublesome thought is.
3. Get permission to remove the thought.
4. Connect again.
5. Add Energy: Bring in Electric violet light through the crown chakra and let it come out of the hand chakras, into the ajna chakra of the patient.
6. Say:

> **"Ajna chakra, seek and destroy all beliefs and thoughts of**
> ....
> **(insert thought to be dissolved) through all bodies through all dimensions, through all time and space. Do this thoroughly and completely. May the energy be transmuted into love and released, now."**
> Ask that they breathe in, and release.

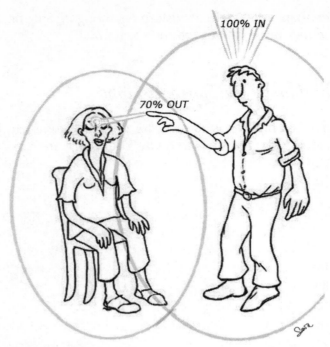

100% IN

70% OUT

Repeat this three times.

Ask them to say:

"I command ....that all supporting thoughts, ...thought forms, ...emotions ....and judgments ....
supporting the thought that (insert) ....
...
.... be dissolved and disintegrated, ...
extracted and expelled............ into the waste bin.......
NOW. In the name of God so be it. Breathe in, release.

7. Repeat this three times.

8. Sweep out the negative energy through the ajna chakra into a bowl of salt water.

9. Ask the patient to think of the floor, or their bedroom, or something bland and unrelated to the issue. Then ask the patient to try to think about the thought you are removing. Say to the patient, "Try to think the thought again." Don't remind them what it was they are trying to remove, by naming what it was! See if it is weaker, or if it has changed on the scale of 0 to 10.

10. If is not gone, repeat steps 4 to 9 again, up to three times, until there is substantial or complete dissolution of the troublesome thought. Repeat weekly for permanent eradication of the negative mental focus.

21. Replace the old thought with a positive one as described below. **Never leave a void.**

Exercise: Building New Thought Forms

After you dissolve a negative thought, it is important to create the opposite, positive thought to the one you just removed. This helps to thoroughly change the mental image, and avoids leaving a vacuum into which the old thought form can return.

1. Devise a positive affirmation that will assist the patient. Ensure it is clear and easy to understand, and do not use ambiguous words. Write it out and modify it until both you and your client are happy with it. Have the finished affirmation in front of you for this procedure so that you can read it.

2. Connect and anchor the violet flame.

3. Bless the patient through the ajna chakra and insert the opposite concept to that which was removed with a positive blessing. In the case of Patricia below it was:

"I am a wonderful, competent person"

4. Get the patient to say:

    (insert opposite concept).......................................
    ....
    ....

    ### *Through the grace of God, so be it".*

5. Tell the patient to breathe in, and Hold. Repeat this three times.

6. Continue the flow of violet flame energy, ensuring that you are only releasing 60-70% of the energy you bring in. Continue until you are aware that there is a lot of energy in the ajna, and stop.

7. To distribute the energy, say:

    ### *'Ajna chakra, distribute this blessing through the whole body, through all chakras and through all dimensions, now. So be it.'*

8. Ask the patient to breathe deeply, and imagine the energy going throughout her body.

9. Seal the ajna to prevent all the energy tumbling out again. Do this by covering it with a cap of blue energy, a gold

criss-cross mesh and a violet flame licking the outside of it. This will serve to keep out contamination before the patient has fully become strong in the new thought.

10. Cut.

11. Give thanks.

"Whatever you want to be, start to develop that pattern now.
You can instill any trend in your consciousness right now,
provided you inject a strong thought in your mind;
then your actions and whole being will obey that thought."
— Paramahansa Yogananda

PATRICIA

Patricia was a lovely woman with many talents and a great personality, but she had always suffered from low self esteem. When she thought of herself it was usually in highly critical terms, and she tended to blame herself for things that went wrong. A habitual thought for her was, "I always mess things up."

There are two levels at which I treated Patricia. Firstly we did an Ignite Your Spirit healing as set out above. Then we did a healing to dissolve the negative thoughts. The first thought we had to remove was that she always messed things up. This was replaced by:

"I, Patricia, am a competent and wonderful person".

Secondly, the huge underlying belief which fed "I always mess things up", was the belief that she was not good enough. So next we focussed on getting rid of this clairvoyantly visible negative thought form. This took a lot longer because it was much deeper and bigger. With persistence, including several repetitions of the healing technique set out below, the thought form gradually lost potency and began to fade. After a few weeks she couldn't believe that she had spent so many years believing such garbage about herself.

Unwanted thoughts can be catching

Since thoughts exist in the watery astral field, they flow around us. When we have a connection with another person, our thoughts can register in their head as well as our own. This is a form of telepathy. It is quite natural, and everyone does this to some extent. Sometimes the last thing we want is to be thinking the same way as someone else. Now, with the violet flame technique, you can *isolate* and clear your mind from the thoughts of others.

KAREN

Karen was happily married to her husband Jim, and had a lovely family. She worked in a legal firm and one of the senior partners, Peter, with whom she was friendly, developed an infatuation for her. He was powerfully attracted to her sexually, and told her so. Karen told him in no uncertain terms that she was not interested, but he persisted (to no avail) with his amorous intentions, and really started to annoy her. The worst part about it for Karen was that she started to feel a very strong sexual attraction to him also. Her logical, rational self was happy and in love with her husband, but it got to the stage that she could not get Peter out of her head.

What I found in Karen's aura was a large thought form of Peter, which was largely the result of contamination from his thinking processes. Since Karen was an open and empathetic person, she had *picked up* his thoughts and emotions.

In one session we were able to dissolve the thought form, which was not even hers, and that was the end of the issue. She was no longer drawn to think about Peter, and she just got on with her life. Because she had eradicated the thought form in her system, Peter also found that his thoughts were less drawn to her and occupied himself elsewhere. They were able to continue with a healthy, friendly, platonic work relationship.

Exercise

1. Work with a partner.
2. Get the patient to choose a thought that originated because of what she has repeatedly been told by another person.
3. Follow the 10 steps of Ignite Your Spirit Healing.
4. Dissolve the troublesome thought form using the techniques set out earlier.
5. Ask your client to say:

    "Isolate............I command...............that all thoughts............ of this nature.........that have come to me from others............be isolated out of my energy field now.........Through the grace of God,.........so be it."

    Breathe in, release.

6. Replace it with a thought that is wholesome and nurturing, and which is the opposite of the troublesome thought.
7. Shield. Build an energetic shield to keep out such thoughts in the future, which can be done as follows:

Place a ball of violet flame energy on the solar plexus chakra, and any other chakra that is involved in the situation. For instance, if there is a matter of a sexual nature, place a ball of energy on the sex chakra. If it is a financial fear, place a ball of violet flame at the base chakra.

8. Fill the aura with violet flame.

9. Will the balls of energy to form into shields across the opening of the chakra, and around the aura. Program the shield with the following:

    "I command.........that these chakras.........and the aura.........be shielded from all negative thoughts,......... vibration,......... energy and elementals.........This shield is semi permeable,.........all negativity can continue to leave.........but none can enter.........Positive and loving energy.........can flow easily into your system............ This shield will last for one week.........So be it."

10. Seal, Cut and Give thanks (as with an Ignite Your Spirit healing).

Shields are not meant to be permanent fixtures in your life, or the lives of your clients. They are like bandages that assist in keeping something healthy while it is healing. The point is to ensure that healing occurs. This happens as we raise our vibration and learn to love whatever it is that was previously a problem. The idea is to become stronger and more robust, and less affected by the negative choices of others. We want to create our own world of happiness, and attract to us others of like mind. If you leave the shield up, you never get to grow through the problem and solve it. You become reliant on the shield, and on staying away from those with negative thoughts, rather than learning and growing from them.

Your best protection from negative thinking is positive thinking and soul connection. This creates waves of energy that flow outwards from your being and affect the world around you.

There are some circumstances where shields are a good idea, and where they may be used for longer periods. If you work in very emotionally and mentally dirty surroundings, such as a mental institution or hospital, it would be a good idea to shield and have regular energy healing so as to minimize the amount of energetic contamination flowing from the sick people. For ordinary use however, shields are for short term application while your consciousness heals.

Mental Health Workers

In Australia, if you are a doctor or nurse in the mental health system, you have to undergo a yearly psychiatric assessment to see whether or not you are still sane. This is because of the incredibly high incidence of mental illness amongst those who care for the mentally ill.

Mental health workers, counsellors, psychologists, doctors and others are at risk from dealing with psychiatrically disturbed patients. The energies that cause the disturbance can readily transfer from patient to therapist, unless the therapist practises energy hygiene and regular cleansing. Symptoms can include: paranoia, belief that people are hiding things, depression, anxiety, inability to relax, insecurity, and so on.

Just like we have a bath or shower daily, if you work in the mental health industry, you ought to do self healing using violet flame on a daily basis. At the very least you should do it every few days, so as to minimize risk of astral contamination.

TOM

Tom is a psychologist whose clients were invariably in a very poor mental state, either psychotic, schizophrenic, bi-polar or suffering from serious illness. Tom did this work for nearly 20 years. He was married with three small children, he worked long hours and was tired and stressed when he arrived home. This put a strain on his family relationships as well as on his own perception of himself. He was also developing depression. Because of the depression which did not respond to anti-depressant medication, a friend of his suggested he come and see me. He had no belief or experience with energy healing, and really only came because he was desperate.

When I looked at him clairvoyantly, I saw that Tom's entire energy anatomy was black with built up grime that he had taken on from clients.

We cleaned up his energy field using Ignite Your Spirit healing, and light started to flow into the chakras again. He came to see me several times and completed our Path of Ease and Grace workshops, so as to broaden his understanding of what it was that had happened, and how he could avoid becoming so contaminated in the future.

After the first treatment, Tom's depression substantially lifted. This physiological change was very evident. Tom was feeling better, and I showed him how to cleanse his own energy field and create shields. We also set up cleansing devices in his office, using crystals, salt and water to keep the space energetically clean.

Tom had been highly professional and detached in his work life. He started to relax more with people, confident that he was safe and aware of how to look after himself. For the first time in nearly twenty years, the psychiatrists with whom he worked thanked him for his efforts, and praised his work. He was radiating good energy, and no longer felt burdened by his work. If he felt some heavy energy coming his way, he isolated it straight away, aware that it was not his.

Etheric Contamination in School children

School children suffer from contamination from other children. There can be thought forms about whether they are good enough, whether they have enough ability, or whether they are sufficiently popular. There can be thought forms about body image, as well as karmic dislikes between students and teachers, and teachers picking on students. Often these negative thought forms are the cause of bullying by others.

Beliefs formed at such a young age are difficult to shift as an adult. We can help our kids by cleaning up their energy field, cleansing negative belief patterns and helping them to develop a habit of healthy self thought. Just as we clean up our own energy fields, we need to look after our children energetically as well.

MICHAEL
Michael was a bright 8 year old in year 3 at school. He got a new teacher at the start of the year, Mrs Jones, who turned out to be the teacher from hell. She took an instant dislike to Michael, and nothing he could do was good enough. Michael had always been well behaved and confident. He started to resist going to school. His mother became concerned but didn't know what the problem was because he didn't want to discuss it. He was often in trouble for not paying attention, and for being late into class after lunch. Then one day he came home in tears and asserted that the teacher had threatened him and told him that he was a nasty little boy. He was clearly terrified.

His mother was tempted to ring the school and complain loudly to Mrs Jones and the school Principal. However, she decided instead that she would treat Michael with violet flame. She cleansed his energy field, cut the cords of energy between him and Mrs Jones, and wiped the fear-filled thoughts from his consciousness. She installed the thought that Michael was a sweet, well behaved and bright boy. Michael felt a lot better, but the proof was in the pudding. How would he go at school?

The following day he went off to school slightly apprehensive. He came home that afternoon with a big grin. The teacher had been nice to him, and he had received a stamp on his hand for good behaviour. He never became particularly close to Mrs Jones, but he got through the year with no further episodes of harassment, and did well socially and academically.

Chapter 17

Renovating yourself with Violet Flame

Some people find that the techniques set out in the last chapter are easier to use on someone else rather than on yourself. It is possible to do self healing to assist your own journey into clarity and stillness of mind. Below are some exercises to help you.

Self healing to dissolve negative thought forms

1. Meditate to raise your vibration before you start. The Archangelic Meditation is recommended.
2. Connect and anchor violet flame.
3. Breathe in through the ajna chakra. Place your left forefinger on your ajna chakra between the eyebrows, and your right fore finger pointing to a bowl of water. You are going to direct all energy out of your body, through the finger and into the bowl. Say:

    "Ajna chakra, I command that you seek and destroy and eradicate from my being all negative thoughts (insert topic, for example, that I am not good enough or that I am not worthy...ment......................) through all time space, and through all dimensions. Through the grace of God, so be it.'

4. Breathe in, release.
5. Repeat several times.
6. Build the opposite thought.

    "Ajna Chakra, accept the program that I am...

    (insert positive loving thought). May this be installed through all bodies, through all dimensions, NOW. So be it.

7. Breathe in, hold.
8. Seal, cut from old self.

9.   Give thanks.

10. Do this daily for three weeks

The more you practice thinking happy thoughts, the less room there is for gloomy and debilitating thoughts. Build yourself a nice strong happy set of thoughts so that they form a positive foundation for your life. When your mind is not being cooperative, it is easier to move on to something that you would like it to think, and which has a positive effect on your energy and ability to love yourself. This is self nurturing and relatively easy to do with practice.

Rubbing out our Mistakes

Have you ever yelled at someone and then wished you hadn't? It is such a shame our mouths do not come with rewind buttons (or at least pause functions!). Many times I meant to say, "ABC" and out of my mouth has come "DEF". Then I think, "Oh my God, did I really say that?" and wish I could take my foot out of my mouth. I feel so sorry but it's too late, the damage is done. The good news is that by using the violet flame, you can actually undo some of that damage.

This practise is a good one to do regularly. At the end of each day, sit quietly and reflect on what has happened during the day. If you get to a part where you said something in anger, or hurt someone, or were indiscreet, you can go back to that time in your mind and apologise to the person concerned. Here is the process in full.

Daily Reflection Technique to Rub out Mistakes

1.   Have a bowl of salt water handy to flick the garbage into.

2.   Invoke.

3.   Connect, and anchor the violet flame.

4.   Review your day from now going backwards, until you come to an incident that you regret.

5.   Think back to what you thought and said. Picture the scene, and who you were with, in as much clarity as possible. Imagine the scene in a small bubble of light in front of you.

6.   Connect to the violet flame.

7.   Fill the bubble with violet flame energy, by bringing it in through your crown chakra and out through your hands,

intending to completely envelope the situation with Divine energy. Then, say

"I now dissolve my negative thoughts, words and actions. May any harmful effect be dissolved and disintegrated, now. May all anger be disintegrated. Through the grace of God, so be it"

8. Breathe in, and release.

9. Rub out what you said by sweeping with your hands.

10. Flick the garbage into the bowl of salt water.

11. Imagine the person in front of you and say, "I am sorry for what I said. Would you please forgive me?"

12. Communicate with them by calmly speaking your truth, in a loving way, so that they can easily understand how you feel. Do this in a way that there is no blame, just observation of what has occurred.

13. Raise your hands with your palms facing outwards, and send love to the person and to the situation. Be aware of your heart chakra. Be aware of your crown chakra and draw in energy through your antakarana. Bring it down to your heart chakra and out through your hands. Imagine it is electric pink energy, the energy of love, and direct it to the person that you have wronged.

14. Ask God to harmonize the situation. Bless the other person and bless yourself.

15. Seal.

16. Cut from the other person, and cut from the work you just did.

17. Give thanks.

Done every day, this is an amazing technique to harmonize your life. It gives you greater inner peace, makes you more mindful, and minimizes any harm that flows from you. It also allows peace to develop in relationships which may have been difficult and challenging.

Healing Anger

In chapter 10 we looked at the effect that anger has on your energy anatomy. You may recall that I said that anger makes the solar plexus become large and the crown chakra shuts down. Let us now test this assertion.

Scan your own solar plexus and crown chakras. To scan your own chakras, imagine you are sitting on a chair in front of yourself, and then scan the'you' sitting in the chair. Many people find this easier than scanning another person.

If you have recently been angry you may find that the solar plexus is very large compared to other chakras, and the crown chakra is relatively small.

If you have not been angry for a while, you can still do this experiment. Scan your crown and solar plexus chakras, and note what you find. Then think back to a time when you were really angry. Put yourself in that time and space, and say, *"I intend to scan my crown chakra and my solar plexus chakra at this time in the past when I was angry."* Wait about 15 or 20 seconds then scan again. Can you feel a difference? Anger swells the solar plexus and shrinks the crown chakra, usually quite dramatically.

The antidote to this is to soothe the solar plexus, and bless the crown chakra. Have a bowl of salt water handy to flick off the garbage.

You can perform this healing on yourself or another person, but for the purposes of this description I am assuming that you are working on yourself.

The first step in this process is to give yourself a complete healing. Proceed with the *ten steps to Ignite Your Spirit*:

1. Invoke.
2. Connect.
3. Perceive.
4. Add energy.
5. Clean.
6. Check.
7. Bless.
8. Seal.
9. Cut.
10 Give thanks.

Now we can specifically treat the crown and solar plexus. Anchor the violet flame and say:

"I now command that all negative energy, all anger and rage be removed from my body, mind and energy field. Through the grace of God, so be it."

Breathe in, release. Repeat 3 times.

Repeat the same affirmation, with your awareness on your solar plexus chakra. Breathe in, and release through the solar plexus chakra. Repeat 3 times.

Sweep the crown chakra, and the build-up of energy from the solar plexus chakra.

Draw in pale blue energy, project this at the solar plexus chakra and say, *"I command the solar plexus chakra to normalize and shrink."*

Visualize it becoming smaller, and being soothed. It is incredible how much better you will feel.

Stabilize and Cut.

Cutting Cords of Attachment

When we associate with others, lines of energy form between us. These lines can become like anchors or chains, binding us to people we might not want to be bound to. This happens between family members and work colleagues, ex-partners, and so on. The more we think about people, the more these lines grow.

Many people going through disputes are shocked to find that they have fat lines of energy joining them to the other party they are in dispute with. By cutting the lines, which is simple to do, we can send back their energy and reclaim our own. Usually when this occurs there are significant breakthroughs in relationships.

Perform the 10 steps to Ignite Your Spirit. Then say:

"I command that all lines of attachment to other people, places, things, times and events that are draining my energy now be broken. I call back my spirit and reclaim my energy, NOW." Breathe in, release.

"I now release all cords of energy that are binding us together. I ask Archangel Michael to help set me free. I cut from you, NOW."

Clean the body where the cords went in. They are often from the solar plexus and navel chakras, but can be anywhere on the body. Some people literally have hundreds of cords attached to different people hanging off them, and wonder why they always feel so tired! Do this a few times, and you will notice a difference.

Working Stress

Workplace stress is a growing and increasingly expensive problem that seems to defy any rational solution. That is because stress is not a rational problem – it is an energy issue. Stress can usually be treated quickly using Ignite Your Spirit healing, and regular meditation will keep it under control. To see how important it is for us to get our heads around this, let's take a look at some research which was done by the Australian Department of Industrial Relations and the Australian Council of Trade Unions within the last few years (see Suggested Readings). The main findings were as follows:

The more stressful the workplace, the greater the likelihood that employees will suffer from fatigue, anxiety, headaches, insomnia, dizziness, panic attacks, depression, cardiac disorders, backache and other muscular syndromes, with a resultant rise in workplace injuries and absences.

There is growing confirmation of the role of stress in heart disease, hypertension, sudden death, skin and gastrointestinal and muscular disorders, and diminution of the immune system. These ailments leave people susceptible to diseases, including cancer.

The Department of Industrial Relations 1995 survey of Australian workplaces found that 50% of employees experienced increased stress in their jobs, 59% reported increased effort, and 46% experienced an increased pace of work. Furthermore, 26% of employees had taken time off work for stress in the previous 12 months.

Stress claims in the public sector alone cost Australia more than $35 million in 2001.

Work cover, the authority that looks after work related compensation claims in NSW, recorded a 10% increase in the incidence of stress at work from 1991 to 1995.

From 1990 to 1994, stress claims in the NSW public sector more than quadrupled from 340 to 1,366. The cost of these claims increased almost sevenfold from $5.6 million to $35.7 million. The number of stress claims in the Commonwealth sector nearly doubled over the four years from 1990 to 1994.

A survey of stress in 2,500 Australian school teachers identified significant workload stress, largely flowing from restructuring, feelings of powerlessness and anxiety. Nearly two thirds of respondents reported implementing new curricula as stressful. Over half the teachers surveyed said that their lack of influence on decisions regarding their work was a major cause of stress. Nearly one in five reported a medically diagnosed stress disorder.

Around the rest of the world, the story is no better. The American Institute of Stress reports that between 75% to 90% of visits to doctors are related to stress, 60% to 80% of accidents on the job are related to stress, and 40% of staff turnover is due to stress at work.

In 1996, the British Institute of Management reported "an estimated 270,000 people take time off work every day because of work-related stress." This represents a cumulative cost in terms of sick pay, lost production and national health charges of seven billion pounds annually. This is equal to the total annual losses caused through theft, and many, many times the cost of strikes.

Health and Safety Executive supplement to the 1990 Labour Force Survey in Britain, found an estimated 183,000 workers believed they had suffered from work-related stress, depression and anxiety in the preceding year. Around 105,000 of these people believed that the condition was caused, not merely made worse, by work.

A 1992 survey of company managers and directors conducted by a British mental health charity, found that 63% believed that problems at work caused as much or more stress for their workforce as personal problems.

A 1993 report by the Warwick Business School's Industrial Relations Research Unit found that hospital staff "privately cite stress as a reason for absence from work, but disguise it as something else to their employers to avoid the risk of damaging their careers."

The Government's response to the increasing number of people experiencing stress at work, has been to make it more difficult to claim compensation for stress. It is not that the Government does not want to solve the problem, it's just that they're looking for the solution in the wrong place. Stress is an energy. If you learn how to clean up your energy, you learn how to manage stress.

Even though a lot of stress might originate from work, it doesn't stay there. Stress, which is fluid, enters the energy field and is brought home. This leads to problems at home such as feeling stressed, being irritable, and the inability to be an active, involved family member because of their preoccupation with work. Bringing work pressures home, is like dumping dirty energy into the family.

Managing Stress

To manage stress the following strategies are recommended:

1. After work, exercise before coming home. If you cannot do this, have a shower and salt scrub as soon as you come in the door.

2. Meditate for 15 minutes twice per day if stress is a serious problem. This will bring peaceful energy to the sufferer.

3. Breathe slowly and deeply when feeling stressed. Let it go.

4. Use a familiar and positive affirmation to help you like, "I am safe and all is well. I am at peace."

5. Use the Ignite Your Spirit self healing techniques set out in this book, or have an energy healing.

6. Use the inner reflection technique to correct issues or poor behaviour throughout the day. Don't just keep going over problems – rub them out.

7. Shield before going to work.

8. Get some training in how to achieve emotional mastery and make constructive use of your mind

9. Take physical care of yourself through proper diet, exercise, sleep and relaxation.

10. Ensure that every day you have some time to yourself, even if it is only 5 minutes. During this time, do not work, look after anyone else or be productive.

11. Take time each week to indulge in your hobbies or creative pursuits. These things feed your energy.

Stress relief treatment

1. Use the 10 steps to Ignite Your Spirit.

2. Say:

    "I command.........that all negative thoughts.........
    vibrations.........emotions ....and all stress.........
    leave my body.........mind.........and energy field now".
    Breathe in, release.

3. Sweep out all the garbage.

4. Anchor violet flame and direct it to the solar plexus chakra. Give it a really good clean, then tell it to shrink. Be calm.

5. Anchor electric pink energy and direct it to the back heart chakra. Ask that your patient be blessed with love.

6. Stress often shows in the crown or base chakras, causing them to shrink. Activate the crown chakra by cleaning then blessing with violet flame.

7. Get the patient to connect to the Earth by doing the Pillar of Light exercise, drawing energy up from the earth into the base chakra.

8. Seal.

9. Cut.

10. Give thanks.

Healing Through Time

Take your awareness back to a time that was very difficult, to one of your major challenges in this life. Do a full Ignite Your Spirit healing on yourself as *though the healing was occurring in the past*. Be aware of the areas where you are depleted or congested, or where there are holes in your aura or chakras. Remove negative thoughts, emotions, elementals and build a positive thought entity which you feed in through the ajna chakra. Ask for a big change for the better to occur through that experience, and that it be healed and cleared rapidly and completely.

You may be aware that you are coming to yourself as an angelic figure back at that time. You may be aware of a danger that passed harmlessly by. This is the effect that what you do now, has on events back then.

Go forward to a time that is coming up in your life that is important to you, that has significance, that you want to feel good in, or that worries you.

Imagine where you will be. Flood the place with violet flame to dissolve and disintegrate all negative energy, negative emotions, negative elementals, all stress energy, all fear and all anxiety. Do Ignite Your Spirit healing on yourself, *at that time*. Ensure that you connect to the Earth to bring in earth energy to support your base chakra.

Flood the place with love by bringing electric pink energy in through the crown and flooding it in to energise the place.

Create a thought form that you are very successful, confident, loving and happy during this encounter. Energise the thought form. Feed it in through the ajna chakra. Send lots of energy ahead of you to make it easy.

Places

Thought forms and energies build up in places. This is why churches feel different to football fields, and why hotels and clubs feel different to places like libraries. Understand that thought forms build-up not only in people, but in places, things, times and events. All of these can be cleansed, and the difference will be very evident. Use Ignite Your Spirit healing to flood spaces or objects with violet flame and sweep them clean. Seal, cut and give thanks. Use the *OM* CD to further cleanse and keep spaces clean.

PART 6
Physical Dimension

Chapter 18

The Physical Dimension

Life on Earth

The physical dimension is the pointy end of a huge multi-dimensional support structure. Having journeyed through the Divine, Soul, Astral and Etheric dimensions, we now land back on Earth. So how do we live here peacefully and happily?

We cannot ignore fundamental physical factors for the enjoyment of physical wellbeing. To look after our physical body we need to eat right, get enough sleep, and do some exercise. All of the mental and etheric cleansing and healing you do may not actually make you healthier if you are ingesting harmful chemicals, or living in a polluted, toxic environment. We are wise to love and respect our physical self and care for our own wellbeing. We are also wise to recognize that the physical world and our physical self is not all there is to look after.

Just like there are spiritual laws, etheric laws and astral laws, there are physical laws. We cannot ignore the law of gravity for instance, or pretend that it does not exist. One only has to step out of a third floor window to see how absolute that law is!

At the same time, much of what we regard as unchanging and immutable is actually just an expression of astral factors, and can be altered. By understanding the vast reality that exists all around us in the other dimensions, we have many tools to draw to ourselves the best things in life. Paradoxically, living in the physical world is much more graceful when we know what lies beyond it.

The power we have to alter life in the physical world through learning more about the 5 dimensions is amazing, and could fill a whole book. In fact, it has. Please refer to my book Dimensions of Wealth if you would like further information.

By expanding our vision of the world and ourselves we can overcome many confronting problems. Remember, we are children of God. We have the capacity to live in harmony, happiness, abundance and peace. If we are not doing so either individually or as a culture, then it is most likely because we actually don't know how.

Take peace for instance. You can't *fight* for peace. As Mahatma Ghandhi said:

"there is no road to peace, peace is the road".

Peace is a state of mind, and a natural side effect of soul consciousness. The likelihood of living in peace and happiness on Earth is enhanced as more people overcome limitations in the astral world and expand into the higher realms of their own innate potential.

Self revelation, and exploration of the different dimensions of our make-up, will bring sustained and lasting transformation to our lives. Any initial realization that we have actually created our experiences and our problems, is rapidly supplanted by the freedom that comes from awareness of how we can change things.

Regular meditation, and practice of the various techniques described in this book will bring you lightness of being and inner strength. Working with the violet flame can change your life, but not if you only just read about it. You actually have to use it! One of the main reasons we are on Earth is to carry out the alchemical process of embodying knowledge through experience. This is a refinement process that takes time, like creating diamonds from coal. Knowledge sits uselessly in our heads until we put it into practice in the physical world and turn it into wisdom. This can only be done through experience.

Like with any new skill, sometimes it helps to be shown what to do. If you want to learn to hit a golf ball and make it go where you want it to, it would help to have some lessons. Spiritual development is no different. It is usually faster and more effective to be shown how to use new tools. We recommend that you attend our Soul Connection seminars so as to experience these techniques with a qualified teacher to guide you.

I wish you warm blessings of inner and outer peace and happiness on your journey into self realization.

Kim Fraser, May 2006

Appendix

Appendix 1: The Chakras

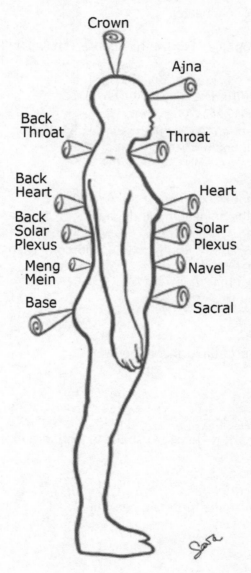

Chakras, Side View

Crown

Ajna

Back Throat

Throat

Back Heart

Heart

Back Solar Plexus

Solar Plexus

Meng Mein

Navel

Base

Sacral

Appendix 2: Suggested Reading

Alice A. Bailey & Djwhal Khul 'The Tibetan'
Esoteric Healing, Treatise on the Seven Rays vol IV
Lucis Press Ltd, 1972 (first publ.1953).

Alice A. Bailey & Djwhal Khul 'The Tibetan'
The Great Invocation
(Found in the front of Alice Bailey's books)

Annie Besant & C.W Leadbeater
Thought Forms
Quest Books,Theosophical Publishing House, USA 1999 (1st publ. circa 1930)

Australian Council of Trade Unions (ACTU)
Stress at Work - Not What We Bargained For
www.actu.asn.au/public/resources/stress/index.html
National campaign launched 1997

Heather Bruce Books
www.heatherbrucebooks.com.au
Amazing images of the antakarana and aura.

Master Stephen Co & Eric B. Robins, M.D., with John Merryman
Your Hands Can Heal You
Free Press, New York USA 2002

Kim Fraser
Dimensions of Wealth
Higher Guidance, Australia forthcoming 2006

Kim Fraser
Ignite Your Spirit
Higher Guidance, Australia 2004
Available through Brumby Books, Australia & Findhorn Press, Scotland.

Kim Fraser
Meditations for Life Enrichment
Higher Guidance, Australia forthcoming 2006/7

Fritjof Capra,
The Tao of Physics
Shambhala Publications, Boston USA, 4th edit 2000

Betsy Chasse
The Little Book of Bleeps: Excerpts from the Award-Winning Movie What the (#$%&) Bleep Do We Know
Beyond Words Publishing, Captured Light Distribution USA 2004

William Arntz, Betsy Chasse and Mark Vicente with Jack Forem
What the Bleep Do We Know!? Discovering the endless possibilities for altering your everyday reality
HCI, The Life Issues Publisher, 2005

Dr Masaru Emoto
Hado.net
www.hado.net/index2.html

David R. Hawkins
The Eye of the I
Veritas Publishing Co. Arizona USA 2001

Christopher Knight, Robert Lomas
Uriel's Machine: Uncovering the Secrets of Stonehenge, Noah's Flood and the Dawn of Civilization
Fair Winds Press 2001

Gopi Krishna,
Living with Kundalini, The Autobiography of Gopi Krishna
Shambhala Dragon Editions, Shambhala Publications Boston & London UK 1993

C.W Leadbeater
The Chakras
Quest Books,Theosophical Publishing House, USA1973

Caroline Myss PhD
Anatomy of the Spirit: The Seven Stages of Power and Healing
Bantam 1997

Caroline Myss PhD
Sacred Contracts: Awakening Your Divine Potential
Random House Australia 2001

Annette Noontil
The Body is the Barometer of the Soul, So Be Your Own Doctor, II
Gemcraft Books Australia, 1994

Dr. Christiane Northrup; Mona Lisa Schulz, M.D., Ph.D.
Igniting Intuition: Unearthing Body Genius
Cassette or CD set, Hay House USA orig. publ 1999

Arthur E. Powell
The Astral Body: And Other Astral Phenomena
Quest Books reprint (orig publ 1927), Theosophical Publishing House, USA

Arthur E. Powell
The Mental Body
Quest Books reprint 1975, Theosophical Publishing House, USA/ India

Elizabeth Clare Prophet
Violet Flame to Heal Body, Mind and Soul
Summit University Press, USA 1998

Elizabeth Clare Prophet
The Creative Power of Sound, Affirmations to Create, Heal and Transform
and other titles by the same author. Summit University Press, USA 1998

Florence Scovel Shinn
The Game of Life and How to Play It
The C.W. Daniel Company Ltd reprint 2004 (orig publ. 1925)

Master Choa Kok Sui
Miracles through Pranic Healing
Institute for Inner Studies; 3rd ed edition Manila, Philippines 1999

Master Choa Kok Sui
Pranic Psychotherapy
Institute for Inner Studies, Manila, Philippines 2000

Master Choa Kok Sui
Meditations for Soul Realization
Institute for Inner Studies, Manila, Philippines 2000

Sri Sathya Sai Baba
Aura of the Divine
The Sri Sathya Sai Books and Publications Trust, India

Barbara and Terry Tebo (with Shelley Neller)
Free To Be Me
Bantam Books Australia 1993

Barbara and Terry Tebo
Free To Be Me - Seminar Notes
Australia

Qala Sri'ama
The Wave
Monthly e-newsletter. To subscribe see website www.g-a-i-a.com or email:
subscribe@g-a-i-a.com

Neale Donald Walsch
Conversations with God: An Uncommon Dialogue: Book 1
Hodder Mobius 1997

Neale Donald Walsch
Conversations with God: An Uncommon Dialogue: Book 2
Hodder Mobius 1999

Neale Donald Walsch
Conversations with God: An Uncommon Dialogue: Book 3
Hodder & Stoughton Ltd, 1999

Paramahansa Yogananda
Autobiography of a Yogi
Self-Realization Fellowship Publishers, USA 1979

Paramahansa Yogananda
The Divine Romance: Collected Talks and Essays on Realizing God in Daily Life
Self-Realization Fellowship Publishers, USA 1996

Paramahansa Yogananda
The Wisdom of Yogananda - SRF Diaries
Self-Realization Fellowship Publishers, USA 2005/06

Gary Zukav
The Dancing Wu Li Masters : An Overview of the New Physics
Bantam; Reissue edition 1984

About the Author

Kim Fraser was a successful barrister for 16 years. She is a spiritual teacher and founder of the Harmony Centre, a charitable life enrichment centre located in Cooranbong near Sydney, Australia. Kim combines an analytical mind with highly developed awareness, intuition and clairvoyance. Fifteen years of passionate study, analysis and experience in spiritual and metaphysical fields, and combining the best and most useful parts of logical and intuitive awareness, gave birth to the Path of Ease and Grace seminar series, a series of meditation CDs and several books, the first of which is called *Ignite Your Spirit*.

Kim teaches in the United Kingdom, India and throughout Australia, to awaken intuition and expand the consciousness of her students. She helps people to access a richer and more fulfilling life, and to touch the heart of their own Spiritual nature. She says:

"In my opinion, the essence of Spiritual teaching is love.

Good Spiritual teaching:

Is not shrouded in mystery and complexity,

Does not defy common sense, incite judgment, nor is it

fear based.

Recognizes that there are many paths to God.

It is easy to understand, effective, reliable, and useful.

Helps us to develop inner strength, tolerance, compassion and good humour.

Improves the quality of our lives, and provides us with self empowerment, understanding, effective and peaceful strategies for conflict resolution.

Infuses us with happiness and appreciation for the richness of life.

Is based on sound universal principals and is relevant to the Age and consciousness of the society in which we find ourselves and resonates with the very core of our being!"

Kim has studied meditation and spirituality with several enlightened teachers from various traditions. She is now able to transmit spiritual energy to help others to discover their own higher guidance, inner peace and self love. This leads to amazing life breakthroughs including better relationships, better health, greater intuitive ability, and a richer life in every sense.

Ignite Your Spirit

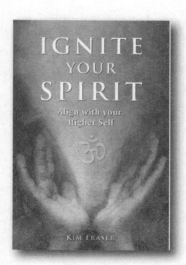

If you want to overcome separation, anxiety, dissatisfaction, loneliness, self sabotage, poor relationships with others, exhaustion, health problems and depression, you need to ignite your spirit. Explore your own spiritual development, and find more to love about life.

Kim's first book *Ignite Your Spirit*, and the seminar by the same name, introduce you to your etheric body and all of the wonders and promises that are held latent within it. You are taught simple and powerful tools to help you live a more successful and grace-filled life. You receive healing, activation, information, stories, life enrichment skills and you have a great time!

Ignite Your Spirit has opened the door for thousands of people to achieve happiness, spirituality and well-being.

Ignite Your Corporate Spirit

Kim has developed a state-of–the-art culture and leadership program which is very powerful and effective. She is able to diagnose your business and assess its strengths and weaknesses in an hour. Using intuitive tools, she can tell you the most insightful and helpful things about where your business is losing energy. She can also mentor and assist you to rapidly transform the energy and bottom line of your company. She works with CEOs, partners in service organizations and board members for maximum effectiveness on a strictly confidential basis. To learn more see www.igniteyourspirit.com or contact our office on info@kimfraser.com

The Harmony Centre

Kim is the founder of the Harmony Centre, located in pristine Australian bush land near Sydney where she holds workshops, teaches meditation and guides others on their spiritual journey. The Harmony Centre is a charitable institution where all seminars and classes are offered by donation. Don't visit if you want your life to stay the same!

Open to the magnificence of your potential in a nurturing space filled with the best that nature has to offer.

Other products and seminars by the author

The Archangelic Meditation CD with music by award winning composer Geoffrey Russell, introduces a powerful process to help you overcome obstacles which may be present in your life, and to experience transcendent bliss. It is musically rich and energetically profound. Regular practice of the meditation will bring to your life more joy, progress and inner peace as you continue on your spiritual journey. This guided journey with the Archangels has six different meditation experiences that can be done separately or all together as a deep healing journey. Available in English, French, German, Italian, Portuguese, Spanish, and forthcoming in Mandarin, Slovak and Russian.

OM is a sacred sound which alters vibrational energy fields, and can be used for cleansing clearing, healing and creating. The melodious chants on this CD cause strong sound waves that can alter your consciousness and merge you with the Divine. Use it to clear yourself, or your home or office.

This double CD set contains two powerful spiritual practices which will cleanse your energy field and bring healing to the physical body.

Dimensions of Wealth

In this workshop and forthcoming book, you will be guided through tested methods for manifesting. You will receive powerful activations to jet propel you out of any negative energy patterns you may have concerning money. Come with a notepad, pen and an open mind and heart. Learn how to:

- Assess your energetic money earning potential
- Increase your money earning potential and grow spiritually at the same time
- Learn about your multiple destinies
- Magnetize to yourself your highest destiny
- Use the laws of the five dimensions of wealth.
- Learn the spiral path of wealth creation
- Learn the difference between yin and yang manifesting
- Appreciate 'the matrix' and how it could be costing you a fortune
- Recognize your own self-sabotaging beliefs about abundance.
- Magnetize to yourself opportunities, luck and prosperity.
- Perceive how karma and other spiritual laws affect your finances, and what you can do about it.

Magic awaits you as you open to material and financial abundance in your life.

Advanced Workshops

The world is a magical place of wonder. Understanding it from an expanded perspective can bring great happiness and empowerment. These are advanced workshop suitable for people with a genuine desire to move beyond themselves and embrace sacredness, the elements, the ascended masters, light body technology, and insight into the subconscious, the astral world and the soul.

Learn how to commune with your guides with discernment and love. Learn about the triple energies of love, light and power. Deep meditations, activations and spiritual practises help you to break through a range of disempowering habits, and achieve incredible clarity of mind. These workshops are never the same twice as it arises from the consciousness and energy of the class which gathers to experience it. Participants report powerful and amazing breakthroughs during and following advanced workshops. Fasten your seatbelt for this one.

Prerequisites for these seminars are Ignite Your Spirit, Dimensions of Wealth, Soul Connection, and regular meditation.

For a complete update on all seminars and products by Kim Fraser, please visit our website www.kimfraser.com